T0274142

The Hustle Cure

Sophie Cliff

THE HUSTLE CURE

A New Approach to Burnout and Productivity for Women

Published by Blue Star Press
PO Box 8835, Bend, OR 97708
contact@bluestarpress.com
www.bluestarpress.com

Interior Design by Brielle Stein
Cover Design by Bryce de Flamand
ISBN: 9781958803806
Printed in China
10 9 8 7 6 5 4 3 2 1

DISCLAIMER:

This book is for informational and educational purposes. This book is not intended to be a substitute for the medical advice of a licensed physician. The reader should consult with their doctor in any matters relating to their health.

The information in this book is not intended to treat, diagnose, cure, or prevent disease. This book is not sponsored or endorsed by any organization or company. The information in this book is based on experience and research done by the author. Neither the publisher nor the author accepts any liability of any kind for any damages caused, directly or indirectly, from the use of the information in this book.

Client names and identifying details have been changed to protect the privacy of the people involved.

For Seren

Table of Contents

Cont.

INTRODUCTION

When you're faced with a big, overwhelming moment, what's your default coping strategy? Do you call a friend? Head out for some fresh air? Write in your journal? Or perhaps, like me, you find yourself standing next to the fridge, panic-eating snacks.

I've been known to dabble in all these approaches, but my default solution has always been books. Throughout my life—whether navigating a bereavement, a career change, or a new stage of life—other people's words have been there to guide and comfort me. And whenever a friend is struggling, I always have a book to recommend—you're much more likely to get a paperback in the post from me than a bouquet of flowers.

So, when I found out I was pregnant in the summer of 2022, it was no surprise that the first thing I did (after staring in disbelief at the test with my husband for at least an hour) was to start adding books to my online shopping basket. But they weren't baby-related books like *What to Expect When You're Expecting* or *Expecting Better* that I was frantically ordering. No, the first place I turned, upon realising that our lives were about to change forever, was the productivity and time management genre.

When I pictured life with a baby, one question kept running through my mind: How will I manage it all? I'd worked hard to build a successful career that was finally blooming. I was working with dream clients and writing for magazines I'd read since I was a teenager, and I was just about to publish my first book. But I was doing it alone. As a solo business owner, I had nobody else to shoulder the burden, nobody else to pick up the reins while I headed off on maternity leave. And it felt like everybody I shared my news with was so keen to tell me about just how much my life would change and just how little time I'd have once our little one arrived. I'd longed for a baby, but now that I was lucky enough to be expecting one, I couldn't stop worrying about the logistics of how I'd make it work. My life was already full, and it was about to get even fuller. Something would have to give.

Desperate for answers, I turned to the experts. I devoured every book I could find on productivity and time management: *Atomic Habits*, *Essentialism*, *Make Time*, *The 5am Club*—all the classics. I binged podcasts promising to help me become my best self, and I followed influencers who swore their tried-and-tested routines would save me time and energy. I watched countless YouTube videos and clicked on every article I could find. I even splurged on a productivity journal that guaranteed to help me get on top of my schedule.

Overnight, I became a scholar in the art of getting things done, poring over every bit of information I could find during those tentative and exhausting early weeks of pregnancy. And while I picked up a few useful tips, two realisations quickly dawned on me. First, these books weren't written by or for people like me. Most were written by men—in fact, when I'd made my purchases, the only books written by women in Amazon's Business Time Management Skills chart were about batch cooking . . . really—and the majority of those men appeared to be key players in the corporate or start-up world, with a vast abundance of resources to support them in their quest for productivity. Their advice, while solid, often felt difficult to apply to my life and situation. There was also a glaring absence of content addressing the specific burdens women face. I couldn't find guidance or tools related to the conversations my friends and I were having about mental load, society's expectation for women to "have it all," or the daily fluctuations in our hormones that affect our lives. All those factors significantly impact our productivity levels, but I couldn't find any resources that acknowledged them.

My second realisation upon reading these books and listening to those podcasts was the pervasive sense of seriousness and heaviness. There was a strong emphasis on willpower, determination, and hustle, or on having a flawless "system" to support productivity. The assumption seemed to be that we could treat our human selves like machines, an idea that clashes with my life's work, which is rooted in joy and helping people find more of it. The time management and productivity world appears to operate under the accepted notions that the sole objective is to accomplish more and that success is defined by achievement alone. But shouldn't we focus on doing more of what enriches our lives? This aspect seemed largely unexplored, and I wondered why.

Productivity has been a topic of discussion for centuries, examined from many perspectives—evolutionary biology, technology, morality, and mindfulness, to name a few. Check the list of nonfiction bestsellers in any given week, and there will be at least one book in the time management and productivity genre. Yet, as I discovered, much of the existing literature still feels lacking. Maybe it's because the landscape has evolved so rapidly in a relatively short time, with more women in the workforce than ever before, technology advancing at breakneck speed, and the pressures we face continuing to mount. Maybe it's because until relatively recently, we've been inviting only one type of person to the conversation on productivity, meaning that a whole chunk of lived experience is being missed. I couldn't find myself or the challenges I face reflected in those books I read, and conversations with friends and clients revealed that they felt the same way.

This is a crucial point to consider because the content we consume—whether through reading, listening, or watching—shapes how we perceive ourselves. When we don't see our realities mirrored in what we consume, we may begin to believe that we're doing something wrong or need to be fixed in some way. I know this firsthand because it has been my lived experience.

I've been reading books like the ones I described earlier since I was a teenager. I remember scouring the personal development shelves at the library, eagerly bringing home my latest finds each week. As I grew older, I filled my own bookshelves with similar titles. Every time I purchase a personal development book, I crack the spine and dive in with gusto, highlighting paragraphs and bookmarking exercises to revisit later. I create plans to help me implement the tips and strategies, convinced that this will be the method or routine that finally enables me to make a change. I start ambitiously, full of energy and optimism.

And then, inevitably, I fail. I end up hitting the snooze button because waking up at five a.m. feels like an impossible feat. I spend so much time trying to categorise my to-do lists perfectly that I run out of time to actually accomplish anything off them. I map out a new, seemingly "ideal" routine based on expert advice and throw myself into following it, only to abandon it a few days later when I realise it's incompatible with my messy, chaotic real life. Each time I've tried and failed, I've internalised that failure as a reflection of my character. I've told myself that I'm too lazy or too weak or too unmotivated. I've berated myself for not wanting it enough. I've felt ashamed that even with someone providing me with a blueprint, I still couldn't make a change. Perhaps you've had a similar experience.

I don't know what was different in the summer of 2022. Maybe it was the years of coaching experience under my belt and the knowledge that I wasn't alone in struggling with this stuff. It could have been that the experiences I was seeking to read about were so obviously lacking. Or perhaps it was the fact that my body was busy growing another human and it no longer felt accurate to label myself as weak or lazy. But as I read those books and failed to find anything that related to my life in their pages, my frustration shifted away from myself. Instead, I grew frustrated with the notion that only a small subset of society is deemed qualified to be productivity experts. I felt frustrated that these books seemed to ignore our inherent humanness—the ebbs and flows of energy, the curveballs life throws at us, and the reality that sometimes, no matter how hard we try, we can't rely solely on determination or willpower. I was frustrated by the superficial view of productivity that pervaded the literature, with its heavy emphasis on doing and far less attention given to exploring what we actually want to achieve.

One question kept nagging at me: Why isn't anybody writing books like this for people like me? For those juggling numerous responsibilities, unlikely to ever perfect a flawless routine? For the ambitious and driven people who refuse to sacrifice their joy? For those who want to get stuff done but don't have the same level of energy every day? For the people who've tried all the gimmicky strategies and are looking for something that will work in their messy, chaotic, imperfect lives?

I searched far and wide for that book but came up empty-handed. So instead, I decided to write it myself.

Let Go of What You've Been Told

I want to start by cautioning you that this isn't your typical productivity book. You won't find any encouragement to push through and hustle until every item is checked off your to-do list. There won't be advice on how to multitask more effectively or on which calendar-blocking technique will help you squeeze the most out of your day. I won't be regurgitating typical productivity mantras like "The choices you make are a vote for the person you want to be" or "You need to work smarter, not harder." In fact, I urge you to actively forget as much of that rhetoric as you can—I know it's easier said than done, when we've been absorbing it both consciously and subconsciously for so long.

Instead, this book aims to help you gain a deeper understanding of yourself. It will guide you in exploring your relationship with productivity and uncovering the origins of your beliefs about getting things done. It will acknowledge your unique circumstances, the pressures you face, and the various responsibilities you're juggling and allow you to see why perhaps you have struggled with making changes in the past. This book will provide you with the tools you need to define success on your own terms and to clarify what will add more joy to your life, empowering you to feel motivated by your own authentic desires rather than hustling to achieve someone else's goals. Most importantly, it will help you embrace your strengths, connect with your intuition, and harness your energy in the way that works best for you.

I wholeheartedly believe that the best approach to productivity is to accept that we are all entirely unique individuals. Doesn't it make more sense to celebrate that uniqueness and use it in your quest to accomplish more rather than to waste your limited energy trying to be someone you're not? Isn't it more logical to focus your efforts on the things that will bring more joy to your life instead of burning yourself out trying to keep pace with someone else's to-do list?

If you're like me, you've probably tried the old way of doing things and found that it didn't work well for you. It's time to try a different approach. Let's abandon the notion that someone else has all the answers and instead start harnessing our own unique brand of magic.

A Note on Whom This Book Is For

It would also be remiss of me not to be bold in my acknowledgement that this book is written primarily for women, as well as nonbinary people who may experience many of the same challenges. I made this choice because having worked with people of all genders in my coaching practice, it has become clear to me that the load women and nonbinary people carry is significantly different from that of our male counterparts. While we will face many of the same challenges, there are experiences that will be unique to us, including sexism, ageism, and the impact of our biology (whether we choose to have children or not), and the expectations placed on us by society and our communities are often greater. I wanted to create a space for us to acknowledge those experiences and understand how they impact our relationship with productivity and our quest for achievement. My hope is that by focusing specifically on the challenges that women and nonbinary people face, we can start to open up the conversations around productivity in a way that feels more inclusive.

Throughout the book, I share examples of my own lived experiences as well as those of my clients. For that reason, it is also important for me to acknowledge the privilege that I have. I write from the perspective of a white, cis, able-bodied woman, and I know that my experiences and opportunities have been shaped by those privileges. I have strived to make this book as inclusive as possible, but if at any time what I'm writing doesn't feel true to you and your reality, that's okay. Whenever I read a personal development book these days, I keep a little mantra in my head: *take what's useful and leave what's not*. Please feel free to borrow that mantra as you delve into these pages.

As you will hear from me many times in the chapters that lie ahead, there is no one right way to do anything in life, only the way that feels right to you. I hope that this book will provide not only new perspectives on the topic of productivity but also tools and exercises that will help you consider your reality and your needs so that you can start to make the changes that feel most joyful and meaningful to you.

How the Book Is Organised

This book aims to explore a fresh approach to productivity—one that is more accessible and human-centric. One that not only recognises our unique qualities and quirks but also helps us use them to our advantage. This approach allows us to embrace our flawed, imperfect, and sometimes chaotic selves without feeling guilty or ashamed. Most importantly, it promotes a more intentional, joyful, and impactful way of being productive.

My training in positive psychology has demonstrated that when we embrace our strengths and pursue our goals in a way that aligns with our values, we significantly increase our chances of success. Hundreds of hours spent coaching brilliant individuals have shown me that there is no one-size-fits-all approach to productivity. Moreover, my own personal experiences have proved that when we start to let go of everything we've been taught about productivity and time management, we can uncover a far better way of doing things. Throughout this book, I'll interweave insights from positive psychology, case studies from my clients, and my own lived experiences to help you figure out how to get everything done in a way that works for you.

In Part One, we'll assess our relationship with productivity and begin to reframe it. We'll explore the origins of our relentless desire for productivity and examine how the constant pursuit of more affects our joy and well-being. We'll then define our own versions of success and determine what "enough" looks like for each of us, shunning unhelpful expectations in the process. Additionally, we'll delve into the role of rest in enhancing productivity, exploring the different ways we can recharge and why they're so important.

Part Two will focus on the importance of doing things your way, and I'll equip you with the tools you need to achieve this. We'll examine our natural energy cycles and explore how we can harness them to boost productivity, focusing on how things like our hormones or sleep preferences can impact us. We'll also explore why leveraging your strengths might be the superpower you never knew you had and discover what flow and balance look like for you.

Finally, in Part Three, we'll dive into The Joy Method—my tried-and-tested model that will help you break free from the rules and prescriptive productivity schedules you've encountered before. Instead, you'll learn to embrace productivity in a way that feels joyful, fulfilling, and meaningful to you. Since this whole book is about making productivity work for you, I'll also guide you through how to personalise the method to suit your life and priorities.

To help you apply the concepts and ideas shared in this book to your own life, I'll introduce you to the productivity archetypes in Chapter Two. There are four productivity archetypes—the doer, the perfectionist, the dreamer, and the procrastinator—and they have been developed from my vast experience supporting clients with all sorts of changes and challenges. Once you identify which productivity archetype resonates with you the most, you'll find personalised tools and suggestions throughout the book that will help you take action, regardless of your style or preference. You'll also come across recurring breakout sections designed to ensure that you put everything you've learnt into practice. The Try This sections will provide practical exercises for you to try, while the Let It Go sections will inspire you to release anything that doesn't serve your desire for joyful productivity, whether it's an expectation or an unwanted chore. Finally, the Do It Your Way breakouts will remind you that there's no one-size-fits-all approach to productivity and planning.

My deepest hope is that by the time you've finished this book, you'll be able to shake off the feeling that you're falling behind or struggling to keep all the plates spinning. I hope that when you turn the final page, you'll feel more confident, more optimistic, and more determined to fill your life with joy.

The days of endless hustle are over. It's time to do things differently.

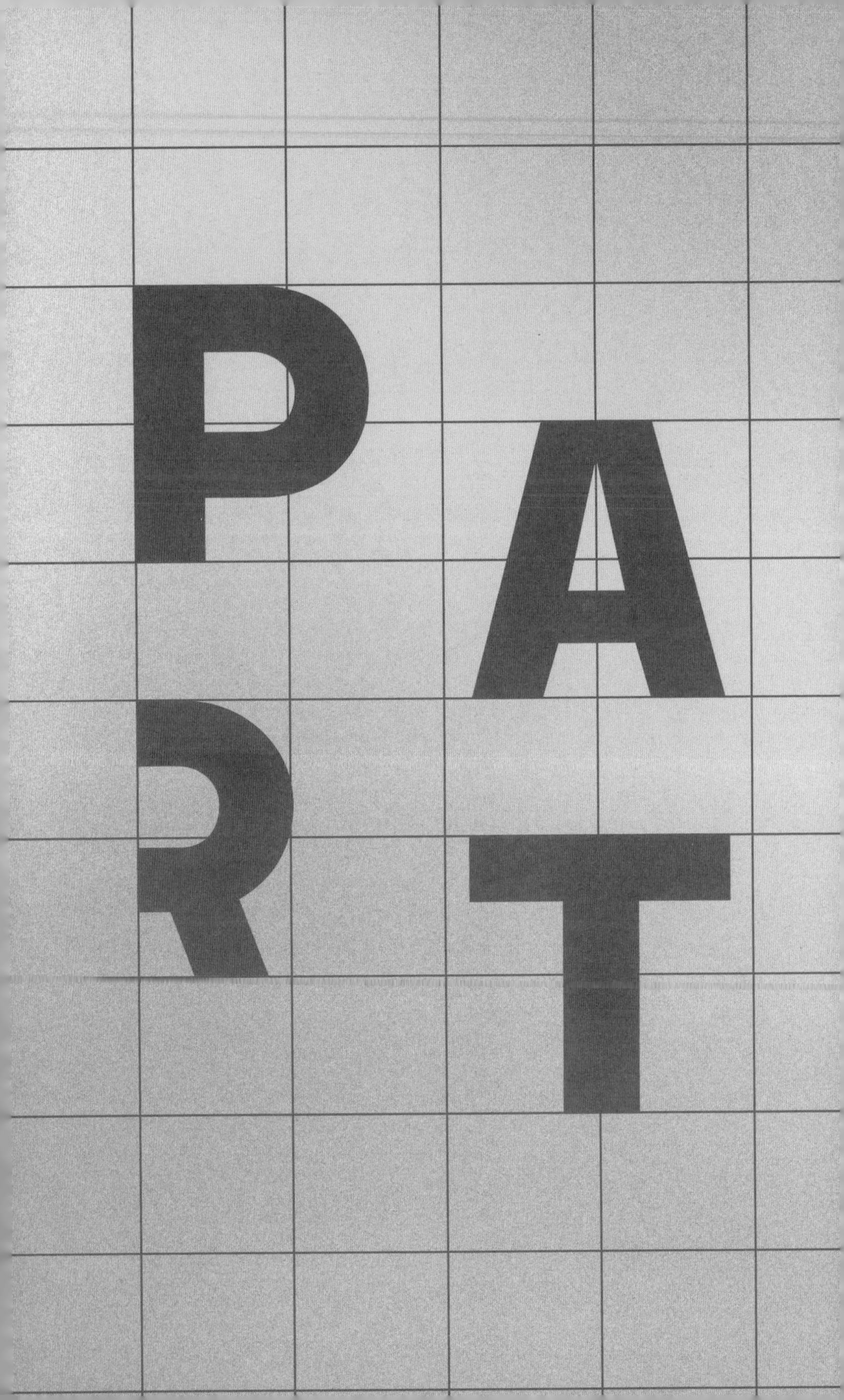
PART

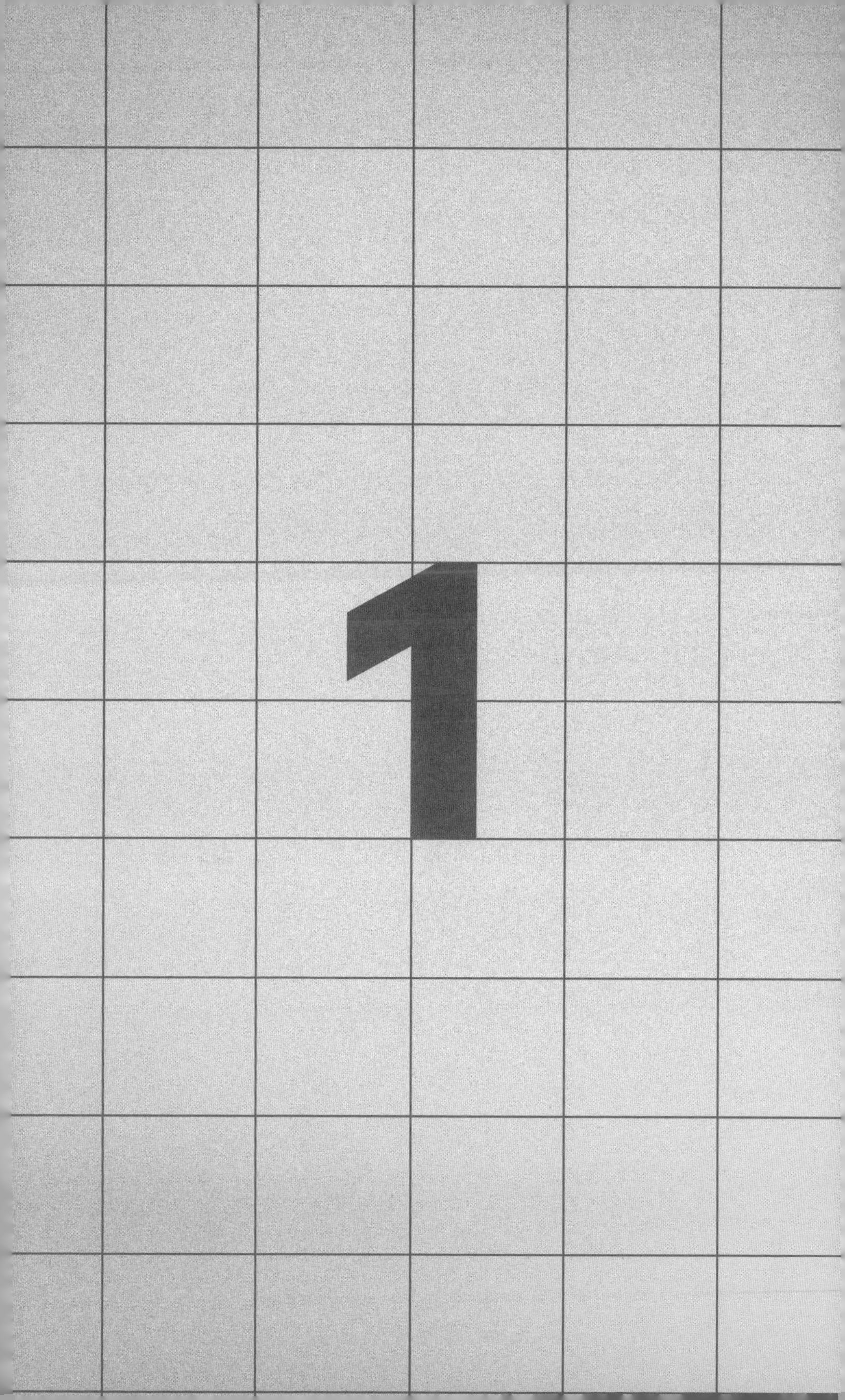

CHAPTER 1:
AVOID THE PRODUCTIVITY TRAP

A couple of months ago, I found myself sitting around a table in a bustling restaurant, eating brunch with some of my oldest friends. We were having a long-overdue catch-up—being scattered across the country means that while our WhatsApp group is always pinging, our in-person get-togethers are far less frequent than any of us would like. As I began to dig into my meal and took in the faces of the people who have witnessed some of the biggest moments of my life, I realised something: in the hour we'd spent together, all we'd talked about was how busy we all were.

These are people whose lives are intricately woven with my own. What I really wanted to know was how their dad was recovering from his surgery or how their daughter was doing at school. I wanted to hear all the details of their most recent trip and ask them what they made of the latest political drama. I wanted to reminisce about the funny stories from our pasts, share in-jokes, and squeeze their hands. I'd waited months to be back in the room with some of my very best people, to catch up on the stuff that was most important to them, to hear their wise and interesting perspectives, and yet it felt like all we'd managed to do was compare to-do lists and talk about how exhausted we all were.

It wasn't intentional. I don't think any of us turned up to that brunch date planning to use our precious time together to talk about how busy we all were. We had just become so completely and utterly consumed by the seemingly endless pressures that came with being women in our thirties that we had little energy left over to think or talk about anything else. And so, instead, we talked about how exhausting it is to remain ambitious at work while also keeping track of our children's social lives and making it to day care pickups on time. We apologised for forgetting one another's birthdays and vowed to try to get together more in the coming months, before struggling to actually pin down a date in our already-jam-packed calendars. We compared ourselves to the peers we'd graduated with and the women our age we followed on social media, wondering out loud how everybody else seemed to somehow be doing it all. We spoke about how difficult it was to make it to the gym these days and how guilty we felt for not taking proper care of ourselves.

We were all so overwhelmed with trying to manage the physical and mental loads we were carrying, so desperate to see if our friends felt the same way and whether they had any tips to help us, that it was hard to cut through the busyness and get to the important stuff. And I think that's a good metaphor for how many of us feel day to day—like there is so much to organise and achieve and get done that there is simply no room for the stuff that really matters: the stuff that brings us joy.

Discovering what brings us joy and considering why we're so often lacking in it are two of the most common themes I explore with my clients in my work as The Joyful Coach. During our first session together, clients frequently express their longing for more joy in their lives and their desire for positive change, but they feel overwhelmed and unable to find space for it amidst their countless obligations. They've tried various strategies—time blocking, rescheduling, waking up earlier—and have followed all the popular advice, but the elusive balance between managing their responsibilities and having enough time for joy still feels like an impossible equation. I deeply empathise with their struggle because I've been there myself. Too many times, I've found myself overcommitted, with a jam-packed schedule that leaves little room for the things that truly matter.

This past year, I've felt that pressure more acutely than ever. Since becoming a mother, I've found my time has never felt more constrained. Despite the immense privilege I have in terms of flexibility as a self-employed person—and the unwavering support of my husband, who takes on more than his fair share of the domestic responsibilities—integrating the care of a whole new person into an already-full life has stretched me more thinly than I could have imagined was possible. The things I cherish most—quality time with my daughter, creating memories with family and friends, spending time in nature—often feel impossible to squeeze in amongst the ever-growing to-do list, the looming deadlines, and the mental load of keeping a little one fed, clothed, and entertained. And I know I'm not alone. Over the course of one week, I had a client tell me that she struggled to enjoy her beautiful beach vacation because she was worried that by taking a break she'd be falling behind with a work project, and another confess that she felt guilty that she couldn't be fully present for her friends in the way she wanted to because her mind was preoccupied with the operational logistics of running a busy household and holding down a job. It seems like we're all feeling more overwhelmed than ever, and it's taking a toll on our joy and happiness.

Since you picked up this book, I imagine that resonated with you. We've been sold the idea that productivity is the solution to our problems, that it's the key to finally managing the never-ending load that we, as women, often carry. We're led to believe that joy is waiting for us just beyond a new routine or approach. But what if, in reality, the relentless pursuit of productivity is pulling us further away from our true priorities? What if, by constantly trying to do more and be more and achieve more, we're actually sacrificing the very things that matter most—our joy, our connections, our well-being? What if by pushing ourselves to meet societal expectations and keep up with our male counterparts, we're ignoring the things that can help us perform at our best: our own energy cycles and unique strengths? What if, to accomplish our goals while also finding more joy in our lives, we need to approach things differently?

How Did We Get Here?

The notion that increasing our productivity will create more time for the things that matter isn't a novel concept. In 1930, the economist John Maynard Keynes proposed that boredom would be the greatest challenge faced by his grandchildren and great-grandchildren. He predicted that by 2030, our typical workweek will be reduced to just fifteen hours, assuming that as living standards improve and technology advances in labour-saving ways, people will opt to work less and enjoy more leisure time. Essentially, he envisioned a working pattern of a two-day workweek and a five-day weekend, the reverse of what we've grown accustomed to. Put simply, he was optimistic that by enhancing our productivity, we'd have more time to spend on the activities we enjoy (1963).

The conditions that Keynes predicted would be necessary for this shift—economic growth, rapid technological advancements, increased global productivity—have all been met or surpassed. Yet we find ourselves feeling more overwhelmed than ever before. Instead of reducing our working hours or carving out more time for rest, our increasingly capitalistic society has necessitated that we use the advances of the past century to cram even more into our schedules. It appears that as our opportunities for productivity have expanded, we've simply demanded more of ourselves.

Technology, for instance, may streamline certain work tasks and save us time in other aspects of our lives, but it has also introduced additional pressure to be even more productive. Social media is a prime example of this. How often have you opened Instagram only to be inundated with posts from the people you follow sharing their latest achievements, leaving you feeling like you're falling behind in some way? This happens to me often—I'll be happily going about my day, and then, suddenly, I'll start worrying that I'm not setting ambitious enough goals for my business, that my home isn't big enough, or that my fitness routine isn't as challenging as it should be. As a millennial woman, I find it impossible to open Instagram and not be confronted with an announcement, whether it be related to a pregnancy, a promotion, or some other tick on the having-it-all checklist. This sentiment has been captured by a new term, *announcement culture*, coined by British entrepreneur and influencer Grace Beverley. In her 2021 book, *Working Hard, Hardly Working*, she defines announcement culture as "our ever-growing need to announce everything we're doing, therefore perpetuating our anxiety of having 'things' to announce in the first place. We judge our success and that of others on the quantity (rather than the quality) of announcements made." And while technology has definitely created a fertile ground for sharing announcements, I notice that pressure to have something to announce seeping into my conversations with friends too, especially those I don't get to see very often. When we finally get together, it's tempting to present our highlight reels to one another, focusing only on the achievements and accolades that make us feel productive and worthy, rather than allowing ourselves to be vulnerable with one another.

The concept of announcement culture appears to be supported by academic research. A 2017 paper by Bellezza, Paharia, and Keinan found that a busy and overworked lifestyle has become a status symbol used to convey importance in much the same way that expensive cars or flashy designer goods do. The authors concluded that being busy creates a perception that a person possesses human capital characteristics, such as competence and ambition, and that these qualities are scarce and in demand. When someone asks us how we are and we reel off a list of our recent accomplishments or the activities filling our schedules (just as my friends and I found ourselves doing at that brunch date), what we're really trying to convey is that we're important, successful, and valued by others. When you look at it that way, it's little wonder that we're all striving to become more productive and accomplish even more.

But I think there's more to our pursuit of productivity than a desire for status. There's no denying that the real pressures and demands placed on women have exploded in recent decades. I notice this a lot when I speak to my own mum about parenting. While I worry about attachment styles and ensuring my daughter is hitting all her milestones on time, my mum frequently reminds me that when she was raising me, parenting didn't come with the same weight or expectations. There were no books extolling the virtues of different parenting styles, no apps informing you of the different developmental phases your child should be experiencing, and no social media creating a crescendo of comparison.

Women also tend to bear the load when it comes to picking up other family pressures, particularly caring for parents or elder relatives, something that is becoming increasingly common given our ageing population, and often it comes with a whole host of emotional and logistical challenges. You might find yourself part of the sandwich generation earlier than expected, juggling the demands of caring for young children and ageing parents simultaneously. Even if you have siblings, you may discover that the responsibility falls disproportionately on you as the eldest daughter or simply because you are a daughter. Or perhaps you shoulder more of the responsibilities for maintaining familial ties, whether that be shopping for Christmas gifts or arranging trips to visit your in-laws.

Moreover, while there's always been pressure for women to look a certain way, as the volume of aesthetic treatments and procedures available skyrockets, so, too, does the pressure to maintain a youthful, flawless appearance. If you choose to keep up with the ever-evolving beauty standards (which seem to change faster than ever thanks to social media), you can find yourself dedicating hours of effort and significant expense to your weekly beauty regimen. And while adhering to beauty standards might sound like an endeavour driven by vanity, research shows that how we look can impact our employability. One study, for example, showed that hiring managers were more likely to deem the candidates they found attractive as suitable for a role (Tews, Stafford, and Zhu 2009), and another study found that a woman's weight could impact her wages by as much as 9 percent (Cawley 2004). The pressure to look a certain way isn't an indication that we're all self-absorbed—it's yet another consequence of our highly capitalistic society.

And while I'm grateful to belong to one of the first generations of women to have complete career autonomy, there's no denying that trying to stay ambitious while shouldering all these other responsibilities can feel overwhelming. I was told repeatedly that I could be anything I wanted to be when I was growing up, and while this was certainly intended to empower me, I internalised it as a pressure to achieve impressive things and never settle. Achieving our career ambitions can feel even more challenging if we choose to have children and have to factor caring responsibilities and the cost of childcare into our career planning. One survey conducted by the British Chambers of Commerce in 2023 found that two-thirds of women feel like they've missed out on career progression as a result of shouldering more of the childcare responsibilities, adding to a sense of frustration and confusion.

Add in hormonal fluctuations that impact our moods and energy levels, and the constant pressure that women face to appear perfect, loving, and compassionate no matter what they're going through, and you suddenly realise that we're faced with an impossible task. Society often teaches us to be embarrassed or even ashamed about the very real impact of our hormones, making it even harder to confront this reality head-on. Women are expected to give endlessly to others, even when struggling with stress, social anxiety, or depression, leaving little time and space to explore their emotions, needs, and desires. As a result, we often end up ignoring our own well-being or facing burnout or other related challenges.

We've grown up hearing that women can have it all, and we've also been sold the belief that we just need to become a little bit more productive to achieve it. But that's a myth. As the goalposts keep moving further and further away, the expectations of what it means to be content and successful as a woman continue to shift, chipping away at our confidence and self-worth in the process.

Busy Doesn't Mean Happy

The real crux of the matter, the belief that underpins the drive for productivity for so many of us, is the notion that doing, being, and achieving more will somehow make us happier. How many times have you heard someone say "I'll be happy when . . ."? How many times have you said it yourself? I know I've uttered that phrase countless times in my own life. I'll be happy when I get a new job. I'll be happy when this project is finished. I'll be happy when I earn a bit more money. I'll be happy when I'm feeling fitter. I'll be happy when my baby sleeps through the night. I'll be happy when we book that dream trip, buy a new house, or I land an exciting new client.

Yet even when we achieve the thing we're striving for, it can feel like the happiness we anticipated doesn't arrive. I've had many experiences like this myself. New jobs or promotions were significant ones for me when I was climbing the corporate ladder. There was one job in particular that I worked incredibly hard for, dedicating enormous amounts of time to applications, tasks, and interviews, while missing out on friends' birthdays and a family get-together in the process. I can still vividly recall the sinking feeling I had a few weeks in when I realised that I still felt just as unhappy, even with a shiny new job title. I had a similar experience with weight loss—I'd long held the belief that being thinner would make me happier, and I spent months running on cold, dark evenings and avoiding the foods I love in pursuit of that happiness. It was crushing to realise that wearing a smaller pair of jeans wasn't the magic key for my happiness that I'd hoped it would be.

I'm not alone in experiencing this—what I'd encountered was what's called *arrival fallacy*. The term, coined by Harvard psychologist Dr. Tal Ben-Shahar (2019), refers to the false belief that once we attain a goal or reach a certain destination, we will achieve everlasting happiness. Arrival fallacy debunks the myth that "we'll be happy when . . ."

Ben-Shahar argues that we're more prone to experiencing arrival fallacy if we start off unhappy and believe that achieving a big goal or milestone will cure our sadness. When success doesn't make us feel any happier, we can become disillusioned, even hopeless and depressed. We then channel all our energy into reaching a different goal, believing that the next achievement will quell our sadness, and the cycle repeats itself. We can find ourselves locked in a negative spiral, and worse, while pouring all our energy into the next thing we think will make us happy, we often miss out on the joy available to us right here, right now.

Put simply, it's highly unlikely that any single goal or achievement will be sufficient to make us feel content and fulfilled. The idea that there will be some point in the future when we will have it all and will have achieved the coveted "happily ever after" is false, and it's also damaging our happiness in the present too. Because when we're busy chasing the next thing on the list of achievements, we're distracted, and we miss out on opportunities for joy that we'll never get back. That might seem extreme, but if you've ever cancelled a dinner with friends in order to stay late at work or sneakily checked your emails while you were hanging out with your kids, you've probably already sacrificed some of the joy available to you in pursuit of some future happiness that never arrived. If our goal is to be happy, we need to prioritise happiness in the present moment rather than sacrifice it in the pursuit of more accomplishments.

Toxic Productivity and the Rise of Burnout

Arrival fallacy shows us that pursuing more in the hopes that it will make us happier is a false economy, but that's not the only reason we need to reevaluate our notions about productivity. Relentlessly pushing ourselves to keep squeezing in more can lead us down the path of toxic productivity, which occurs when we're so focused on producing that we neglect other important aspects of our lives. If we prioritise productivity over our basic needs, such as rest or quality time with our loved ones, we put ourselves on a fast track to burnout.

Many of us are already there. Research shows that levels of burnout are at an all-time high, with a 2023 Future Forum study finding that 42 percent (and rising) of the workforce reported experiencing it. The same piece of research also revealed that women are at a higher risk of burnout than men (the gender burnout gap has doubled since 2019, potentially exacerbated by women taking on more of the increased mental and domestic load since the pandemic), and young people (those aged thirty and under) seem to be suffering more too, with redundancy anxiety and lack of training causing them to be under greater pressure to perform at work.

What concerns me about these numbers is that it's easy to forget that just because burnout is common doesn't mean it isn't serious. If you've never experienced burnout, you might be forgiven for thinking that it can be remedied with a few bubble baths and an early night, but the reality is that it can be debilitating. I know that when I experienced it back in 2017, it took me months to fully recover, and it left me with so little energy that I could barely manage the essentials required to keep my life functioning. I've supported clients who've experienced similar challenges—one struggled to enjoy her wedding day because she was in the depths of stress-related burnout. Another spoke sadly about how she barely remembers her son's newborn days—she had pushed herself so far to the limits in a rush to get everything done before her maternity leave that she spent the first few months of motherhood wading through an exhausting fog of adrenaline.

We don't talk enough about the impact that burnout can have on our confidence. Experiencing it left me with crippling self-doubt, something I had to spend years working through to finally feel confident enough to pursue my dreams and ambitions. I know I'm not alone in this. I've worked with hundreds of brilliant people who are talented, creative, and motivated but struggle with anxiety or poor self-esteem triggered by a bout of burnout. There's also the shame that comes with having to slow down or stop—things that are seen as weaknesses in our society. It's much easier to focus on what we haven't been able to do as opposed to what we have done, and the fear of falling behind or letting others down can lead us to cut short the recovery period we need. There's a real risk of triggering a negative self-perpetuating cycle: we feel like we're losing control or failing to be productive, which further depletes our energy and optimism, trapping us in a rut that can feel impossible to escape. How ironic that in trying to do more, so many of us find ourselves in a position where we can't actually do much at all.

DO IT YOUR WAY

There is so much more to life than how productive we are. Use the following journal prompts to reflect on the role busyness has played in your life and on who you are outside your achievements:

- What role has busyness played in your life so far?
- How does being busier than you have the capacity for make you feel?
- Have you ever experienced arrival fallacy? Write about what happened and how it made you feel.
- How has society's expectation that women should have it all affected your relationship with productivity and happiness?
- In what ways have you felt pressure to be the "perfect" woman—mother, wife, employee, friend, daughter, or any other role? How has this impacted your mental health, identity, or well-being?
- Have you ever felt guilty for taking time for yourself or prioritising self-care? Why do you think that is?
- Have you ever compared yourself to other women who seem to be doing it all? How did that make you feel, and what do you think might be the reality behind their seemingly perfect lives?
- What is important to you beyond achievements? What makes you who you are that has nothing to do with doing?
- As a child, what made you feel happy? Does looking back inspire any ideas for how you can find more joy as an adult?
- What would improve in your life if you had more time for the things that bring you joy?

A New Approach to Productivity That Honours Your Need for Joy

We can't continue like this, hoping that the next routine or time management hack we try will be the magic solution to our productivity problems, all while sacrificing our joy—or, worse, becoming sick. We can't keep hoping that someone we've never met holds the answers, all while dismissing our own unique needs, resources, and experiences. We've tried doing it that way, and we've only become busier and more burnt out than ever before.

It's time to do things differently. It's time to start trusting that you know yourself better than anybody else and start using that knowledge to help you not just tame your to-do list but fall more in love with your life in the process. I'm not talking about letting go of your ambition. I'm asking you to redefine your relationship with it in a more joyful and intentional way. We've all heard the phrase nothing worth having comes easy, but what if that's wrong? What if finding joy in the journey, and embracing your own superpowers, is the key to success? As I'll share later in the book, research from the field of positive psychology suggests that we should all be doing just that.

We have long believed that the key to productivity lies in willpower, systems, or unbreakable habits. I believe that, instead, the key to being productive while feeling balanced lies in using your strengths, honouring your energy cycles, and harnessing your motivations. Over the course of this book, we'll do exactly that. We'll take a more compassionate and human-centric approach, one that is grounded in your reality, and I'll share tools and ideas from the field of positive psychology that will help you get more done in a way that feels good to you. I'll also introduce you to the Joy Method, my tried-and-tested process that will help you break free of the traditional rules and expectations around productivity and instead embrace a more joyful and fulfilling approach.

But first, I want to invite you to challenge your definition of productivity. Like so many other things in life, we absorb our beliefs about productivity from the society, culture, and environments we grew up in. If you had a mother who never sat still, you probably believe that being productive means always being on the go. If you grew up in a culture that values achievement over all else, you might associate productivity with having a high-status job, regardless of how unfulfilling said job feels to you. If you've ever worked for a boss who sends emails in the evenings or on weekends, you might believe that to be productive, you need to be working at all hours. If you've ever experienced scarcity or lack, you may have absorbed a belief that it's unsafe to slow down and switch off from your to-do list, so you haven't done it even though your life is very different now.

Regardless of the experiences that have shaped you, I invite you to reconsider your method of operating. Because true productivity isn't about how much we can squeeze in or get done. It's about focusing our energies on the stuff that truly matters to us. True productivity isn't about how quickly we can achieve something. It's about finding joy in the journey, savouring the process of working towards a goal or milestone. True productivity isn't about having it all. It's about being intentional in envisioning the type of life you want to have, and then using your unique skills and resources to build it. And, as you'll learn in this book, one of the big payoffs of focusing on joy rather than productivity is that doing so makes you more productive than if you were simply trying to get as much done as you can, because you'll be moving in the direction you want your life to take.

Since you've picked up this book, you probably know, deep down, that the old approach isn't working anymore. Let's try something different.

LET IT GO

We all have unique experiences, environments, and communities that have shaped how we show up in the world. By taking the time to reflect on our beliefs, we can start to identify where they came from and be intentional about whether we want to hold on to them.

Using the prompts below, take some time to reflect on the beliefs you hold about productivity:

- What was modelled to you about productivity when you were younger? For example, how much did you see your parents or caregivers relaxing? Were you rewarded for getting your work done quickly at school, and if so, what was the reward?
- What messages did you receive growing up about what it means to be a "successful" woman?
- Where does your drive to be productive come from? Think about specific triggers that you might have—for example, perhaps money has felt scarce in your life and you believe that if you slow down, you'll be risking your economic security.

- Have you picked up any specific beliefs about what productivity should look like for you as a woman? Is the pressure to look a certain way impacting your beliefs, for example? Or perhaps you feel a pressure to achieve certain things to show other women what's possible.
- How have the various roles and responsibilities you hold as a woman—for example, caregiver, homemaker, breadwinner—influenced your perception of productivity and success?
- Are your beliefs around productivity and joy intertwined in any way? For example, do you believe that you will be worthy of joy only once you've achieved a certain goal?
- Do you have any productivity beliefs that are getting in the way of your joy and happiness? For example, is your drive to be the perfect mum who does it all actually making you less present with your child?
- Have you ever felt pressure to downplay your ambitions or achievements to fit in with societal expectations of women? How has this affected your relationship with productivity and success?
- As a woman, have you ever felt like you needed to work twice as hard to prove yourself or be taken seriously? How has that impacted your approach to productivity?
- Have you ever struggled with the belief that your worth as a woman is tied to your productivity or accomplishments? Where do you think that belief stems from?
- How has the "superwoman" stereotype (the idea that women should be able to effortlessly manage their careers, families, and personal lives) influenced your beliefs about productivity and self-worth?
- Write a list of beliefs that you want to let go of. Then think about the new beliefs you might replace them with. For example, maybe you want to replace "I'll be happy when . . ." with "Joy is available to me right now if I slow down enough to experience it."

In addition to examining how societal norms have shaped our relationship with productivity and success, it's crucial to consider the unique challenges and pressures women face when it comes to how productivity informs feelings of self-worth. This curiosity can help us develop a deeper understanding of how societal expectations and gender roles have shaped our beliefs and behaviours, which in turn can help us practise more self-compassion and embrace a more joyful, fulfilling approach to productivity.

LET'S RECAP

- **Despite advancements in technology, our lives feel busier than ever, and the pressure to achieve is immense. Many of us are struggling to juggle it all, and joy often falls to the bottom of our to-do lists.**
- **In the pursuit of greater productivity, we tend to seek wisdom from external sources instead of embracing our own inner knowledge. As a result, we find ourselves burning out or trapped in a cycle of shame and blame.**
- **Our definitions of productivity are not always intentional, which can hinder us from prioritising what matters most to us.**

CHAPTER 2:

IDENTIFY YOUR PRODUCTIVITY ARCHETYPE

I'm a big believer that the only way we can be productive without sacrificing our joy or risking burnout is by taking a personalised approach. However, I also recognise how intimidating that can be. Our society has conditioned us to seek answers from external sources. From a young age, we are taught to listen to our parents, and then our teachers, and later our bosses. Rarely are we encouraged to look within ourselves for guidance, so if you're feeling overwhelmed at the idea of figuring out what works best for you and your unique circumstances, know that you're not alone. In fact, most of my clients find themselves in a similar position.

Throughout the book, we'll explore various tools and exercises to help you gain a deeper understanding of yourself. To make it easier for you to identify the changes that will be most beneficial, I want to introduce you to the concept of productivity archetypes.

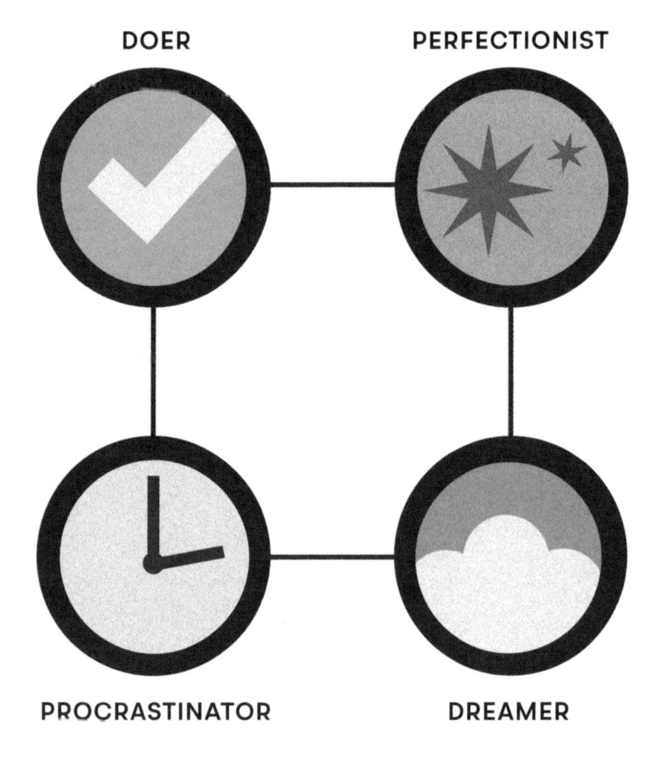

Over the last five years, I've worked with hundreds of clients, supporting them in making joyful changes in their lives. Despite each client's unique circumstances and personality, I've noticed recurring productivity styles or archetypes. These include the following:

- **DOERS:** People who are driven by achievement and always seem to be busy.
- **PERFECTIONISTS:** Individuals who hold themselves to the highest standards and are motivated by doing everything right.
- **DREAMERS:** Those who easily envision a better world but may struggle with turning their dreams into reality.
- **PROCRASTINATORS:** People who want to make a change but find it challenging to take meaningful action.

Each archetype has its own inherent strengths and motivations, and they also tend to have some common pain points or obstacles that hinder their progress. You'll find the detailed descriptions of each in this chapter, and in the remaining chapters of the book, you'll discover personalised recommendations for each archetype.

Of course, it's impossible to capture the nuance and complexity of humanity in just four categories, and you might not feel as though you fully fit into one of the archetypes I've outlined. That's okay! We are all wired in our own unique ways. We have our own motivators that have been shaped by our experiences. I wanted to share these productivity archetypes not to make you feel like you need to reduce yourself to any one label but simply to offer up guidance to help you navigate the tools shared throughout the rest of the book.

I also hope that by reading the descriptions of each archetype, you might realise that you're not alone. We often think that the reason we're struggling is because we're flawed in some way, and that can be an incredibly isolating and shame-inducing experience. I hope that knowing others struggle with the same challenges—as well as discovering some ideas to help you navigate those challenges—will help you feel more confident in taking action.

There are some tools to help you find your archetype later in this chapter, but if no one archetype feels true to you, simply notice which elements you relate to, resisting any pressure to put yourself into a box that doesn't fit. You may also discover that you relate to different productivity archetypes in different areas of your life. For example, you might feel like a doer at work but behave more like a procrastinator when it comes to other projects in your personal life. In short, I've provided these archetypes to help you navigate the tools and concepts in the rest of the book. Try to see them more as loose groupings rather than in-depth prescriptions.

The Doer

First, let's explore the doer. Doers thrive on achievement and love to be busy. They're always working towards a goal or milestone and are known for their ability to accomplish a great deal. Highly adaptable, doers juggle multiple responsibilities with ease and often excel in whatever they put their minds to, thanks to their efficiency and focus. However, sustaining such a high level of energy output means that doers are more susceptible to burnout compared to other productivity archetypes. Many women fall into the doer archetype, perhaps because we have been conditioned to believe that having and doing it all are the pinnacles of success as a woman. Or perhaps some women have had to become doers in order to manage the long list of competing pressures and demands placed on them.

There are many advantages to being a doer, as well as some challenges. Let me share them here:

What are the strengths of a doer?

- Doers are self-starters with a high level of motivation. They don't struggle to take action and can be relied on to get the job done, making them a great asset to have on a team or in a community.
- Doers wear many hats with ease and find it easy to manoeuvre between their different roles and responsibilities—for example, slipping straight into work mode after dropping their child off at day care. This fluidity means that they find it easier to manage the competing demands of work and life than other archetypes.
- Doers are often (but not always) extroverts, meaning they get their energy from being around others. This gives them an advantage in roles or situations that require networking or strong communication skills to get ahead and succeed.

- Doers are reliable and willing to help. They are the friend who organises the annual get-together (complete with detailed itinerary), the parent who is always willing to help at the school bake sale, and the colleague who can be counted on to deliver their actions on time.
- Doers are high achievers—when they set their mind to a goal, they will give what it takes to achieve it. They are determined and proactive, qualities which may have helped them build a life that appears very successful to others.

What challenges does a doer face?

- Doers struggle to acknowledge or accommodate their energy cycles, which means they're at an increased risk of experiencing burnout. Burning out (and having to slow down as a result) can be a source of shame or guilt, which can take a toll on their self-esteem.
- Doers, while they respond well to positive feedback, can sometimes rely too heavily on external validation to feel worthy. They also struggle to celebrate their own achievements and instead find themselves jumping into the next project or goal without taking a beat to reflect or internalise their success.
- Doers, being constantly busy, often miss out on valuable insights and nudges from their intuition. This can sometimes hamper their decision-making.
- Doers struggle to maintain boundaries when others ask for help, often saying yes even if they know they're already at capacity.
- Doers are less intentional and more impulsive than other archetypes. While this can sometimes be a positive (their impulsive actions will sometimes pay off), it can mean that they waste time pursuing goals or opportunities that don't bring them more joy or more of the type of success they desire.
- Doers may also find that the goalposts are constantly shifting, leading them to berate themselves for not accomplishing enough, even as their output and achievement levels continue to rise. Over time, this can contribute to poor confidence.

What is the doer's relationship with productivity like?

Doers are naturally very productive people. They have a high level of output and will likely rack up many impressive achievements. However, doers may lack intention, which means that while they can get a lot done, it might not be the stuff that feels most joyful or important to them. If they don't build in time to pause and reflect, they can be at risk of hustling themselves down a path that isn't right for them, which might not feel quite so productive further down the line.

It's also important for doers to recognise where their drive to be productive comes from. As we discussed in Chapter One, we live in a society that celebrates busyness and output, which can sometimes lead to a belief that being productive will make us seem more important or worthy. Plus, as the demands placed on women increase, many will feel like they have to become doers in order to keep all the plates spinning. However, chasing productivity for productivity's sake is never going to be joyful and fulfilling. The biggest opportunities for a doer are to get clear on what they want out of life and why (more on this in the next chapter) and to use their strengths to help them achieve it—even if that means going at a slower pace.

You'll know you're a doer if . . .

- You start every new year with an impossibly long list of goals that may seem disconnected to your real life.
- You treat big life events, such as getting married or starting a family, as projects to be managed or accomplishments to be checked off a list in a quest to have it all.
- Your calendar is so full that when a friend tries to schedule a catch-up, you suggest a date three months in the future.
- You struggle to relax even on vacation, creating elaborate itineraries and scheduling every moment of the trip.
- Your default coping mechanism when you experience periods of low confidence or self-worth is to distract yourself by doing something.
- You find that you get ill whenever you do slow down (during the holidays, for example).

- You might find it hard or unnatural to embrace nurturing or caregiving roles where the workload is repetitive and of a less tangible nature.

The Perfectionist

Next, we have the perfectionist. Perfectionists are known for their high standards, disciplined approach, and meticulous attention to detail. Perfectionists are highly attuned to the needs of others and may be prone to prioritising being the "perfect" daughter or "perfect" employee over their own joy and fulfilment. Perfectionists can find it challenging to celebrate their wins, which can take a toll on their confidence and self-esteem. They're also very sensitive to criticism or feedback from others, with any suggestion that they aren't achieving perfection feeling incredibly stressful. It's easy to see how many women end up falling into this archetype given the incredibly high standards we hold them to. This is especially true in an age of social media and gossip sites. Perfectionism can often feel like the only safe strategy to pursue in a world where women are regularly torn down for being anything less than perfect.

As with doers, perfectionists have their own strengths and challenges. Let's explore some of them.

What are the strengths of a perfectionist?

- Perfectionists tend to be the most disciplined of the archetypes. They thrive when there are clear rules to follow and expectations to meet and find it easier to maintain a routine than others.
- Perfectionists have a keen eye for detail and the patience to get things "just right," skills that can be very useful in a wide range of settings, from spotting errors in important work documents to curating a warm and welcoming home.
- Perfectionists are incredibly caring and are motivated by getting things right for other people, whether that be their boss or their children. They put a lot of thought and effort into everything they do, from picking out a gift to delivering a presentation at work.
- Perfectionists are conscientious and responsible. They are organised and orderly and can be counted on to do what they say they'll do.

What challenges does a perfectionist face?

- Perfectionists can sometimes get caught up in caring more about how their life appears to others than how it feels to them. In a rush to appear successful or perfect to their peers, perfectionists can end up missing out on joy and may feel like their lives are always lacking greater purpose. This tendency can also make them vulnerable to comparison.
- Perfectionists may believe that there is one "right" way to do something and will spend a lot of time in research mode, exploring and analysing every option. This can sometimes hold them back from seeing that there are many definitions of success and many paths to achieving it.
- Their commitment to a perfect plan can sometimes hold them back from taking action, and perfectionists may struggle to complete tasks and move on to the next thing on their to-do list because they're striving for an ideal outcome.
- Perfectionists can expect themselves to perform at the same level every day, meaning they struggle to listen to their own energy cycles or honour their need for rest. This puts them at risk of burnout but can also mean they aren't always working in the most efficient way.

What is the perfectionist's relationship with productivity like?

Perfectionists have many traits that help them be productive, from their discipline and high levels of motivation to their consistency with routines. However, their desire to get things "just right" may hamper their productivity, leaving them spending large amounts of time on tasks that don't add a proportionate amount of value. Additionally, perfectionists are often driven by the opinions of others rather than their own definition of success, which may mean that even though they achieve their goals, they don't feel as successful and content as they may have hoped.

Just like with the doers, it's important for perfectionists to recognise where their drive to be productive comes from. From a young age, girls are encouraged to be "good," with good meaning following the rules, being presentable, and often putting the needs of others before themselves. This can embed a perfectionist tendency from a young age. Additionally, perfectionism can act as a guard of armour, seemingly protecting us from judgement and shame. However, if we prioritise perfection over authenticity, we are never going to feel joyful and content. The biggest opportunity for a perfectionist is to embrace flexibility. Doing so will help perfectionists better harness their energy cycles (more on this in Chapter Five) and find more joy in the process of achieving their goals.

You'll know you're a perfectionist if . . .

- ✿ You take months to book a vacation because you spend so long researching the perfect hotel.
- ✿ You struggle to make a decision without first polling others for their opinion.
- ✿ You have a clear picture of what a "perfect" woman is and spend a lot of energy striving to be her.
- ✿ You rarely feel like a task or project is done and can always find tweaks or additions that would improve it.
- ✿ You compare your choices to other people's, worrying that you haven't made the "right" decisions about how to parent, where to live, or what career to pursue. The pressure to have it all feels real.
- ✿ You feel resentful when your efforts to be a "perfect" daughter, sister, or employee aren't recognised or reciprocated.
- ✿ You have a drawer full of journals that you've abandoned because you didn't fill them in perfectly.

The Dreamer

Our next productivity archetype is the dreamer. Dreamers are creative and innovative, excelling at imagining and crafting a vision for their lives. New ideas flow to them effortlessly, and they are adept at seeing and articulating the big picture. However, dreamers can struggle with turning their vision into actionable steps and goals. I've found in my work as a coach that there is sometimes a little shame attached to being a dreamer, particularly for women, perhaps because unlike with doers and perfectionists, their strengths and skills are less celebrated in our hypermasculine and output-focused world.

However, they have a lot to offer. Let's explore their strengths and challenges, as well as their relationship with productivity.

What are the strengths of a dreamer?

- Dreamers are great at seeing the big picture. They don't get bogged down in the little details and, instead, are able to focus on the bigger task at hand. For this reason, they are less flappable than the other archetypes and can remain cool in the face of stress.
- Dreamers are fun people to be around, naturally embracing opportunities for play and self-expression. They don't take themselves too seriously, and their approach to life can be inspiring to others.
- Dreamers are creative and innovative and find it easy to look at challenges from different perspectives. They are skilled at problem-solving and generating new ideas and find it easy to tap into their intuition.
- Dreamers are natural optimists, always dreaming up better ways of doing things and hoping for a brighter future.

What challenges does a dreamer face?

- Dreamers can be particularly susceptible to arrival fallacy, buying into the idea that they'll find happiness only once they've brought their vision to life, therefore missing out on the joy available to them in their daily life.
- Dreamers, while great at setting the vision, may lack the discipline and consistency needed to make steady progress. As a result, they may become discouraged over time if they don't see their dreams becoming a reality.
- Dreamers often suffer with low confidence or struggle to see the value in their strengths, particularly if they have been raised in environments or cultures that celebrate skills such as leadership and assertiveness over creativity and innovation.
- Dreamers may struggle with monotonous tasks, making it harder for them to navigate caregiving roles or stay on top of life's "admin," or administrative tasks.

What is the dreamer's relationship with productivity like?

Unlike doers and perfectionists, dreamers often find it easy to define their own authentic definition of success. Having clarity over what they want to achieve in their life means they waste less time pursuing goals that aren't relevant to them and their vision. However, they often struggle to maintain the consistency of action required to turn their dreams into a reality, which can hamper their productivity. Additionally, they may suffer from what I like to call *shiny magpie syndrome*, getting distracted by new ideas and goals before they've had the chance to finish other projects.

One thing that holds dreamers back from reaching their full potential is dismissing their natural strengths. Many dreamers I've supported were told as children that they had their head in the clouds or that they needed to focus more, which means they now downplay the skills that set them apart, skills that could help them build an incredibly joyful and fulfilling life for themselves. If dreamers embrace their strengths and find strategies to commit to their goals (which I'll share later in the book), they can make magic happen!

You'll know you're a dreamer if . . .

- You have Pinterest boards full of new ideas you want to explore or experiences you want to have.
- You're great with kids and may be seen as the "fun" parent or aunt, as you find it easy to match their energy and imagination.
- You love the process of dreaming up new goals and ambitions at the start of a new year (but don't relish the reflective period at the end of the year).
- You sometimes feel guilty for wanting to pursue other passions and interests outside your current family or work obligations.
- You're the first port of call for friends and loved ones when they need a gift idea or someone to bounce ideas around with.
- You always leave a train or plane journey with a notebook jam-packed with new ideas, but you find it hard to focus on the project at hand.
- You struggle with impostor syndrome, especially when working in male-dominated spaces or fields.

The Procrastinator

Finally, we have the procrastinator. Procrastinators tend to be more rebellious and creative than the other archetypes, and they can be efficient when the situation demands it—often working best when faced with a looming deadline. However, they may feel lost and struggle to set goals or carve out a clear path for themselves. This could stem from a lack of belief that things can change or a lack of confidence in pursuing their dreams. In my experience, women tend to fall into this archetype if the demands placed on them feel completely overwhelming, pushing them into fight, flight, or freeze mode, or if they suffer with low self-esteem.

What are the strengths of a procrastinator?

- Procrastinators are often quite risk averse and can be skilled at spotting any potential obstacles or hurdles to success, meaning they conserve their energy for the most productive tasks.
- Procrastinators work very well under pressure—they can get more done the day before a deadline than most people can get done in a week.
- Procrastinators, as research has shown, are more creative than those who don't procrastinate. This is thought to be because they have longer to think over problems and come up with different ideas and solutions.
- Procrastinators are better than all the other archetypes at acknowledging and accepting their unique energy cycles, meaning they utilise their energetic ebbs and flows more efficiently.

What challenges does a procrastinator face?

- Procrastinators often find their biggest challenge is falling into a negativity trap—struggling to take action, then blaming themselves for not taking action, which in turn makes it more difficult to take action, creating a vicious cycle.
- Procrastinators, deep down, sometimes may feel that it's not safe for them to want what they want, and they will seek out evidence that supports this belief.

- Procrastinators can face periods of intense stress or overwhelm if they allow deadlines or priorities to build up. This can be challenging for their mental health and overall well-being.
- Procrastinators may feel a sense of shame or guilt if they can't work in the same way as their peers, which can further damage their confidence and self-esteem.

What is the procrastinator's relationship with productivity like?

Contrary to popular belief, being a procrastinator doesn't mean that you can't be productive—it's simply likely that you take a different route to achieving your goals than the other archetypes. If procrastinators learn to harness their strengths (which we'll cover in much more detail later in the book), they can achieve a great deal and build their confidence in the process.

The biggest opportunity for procrastinators is in realising that they do have what it takes to build a life that feels joyful and successful to them. So often, procrastinators can find themselves locked in a negativity spiral, believing they don't have what it takes and finding evidence to back that up. They might look at other women in their workplace or community and feel a sense of shame that they can't focus in the same way, but procrastinators have their own superpowers, and when they embrace and engage with them, they can make real positive change happen. The first step is to believe that.

You'll know you're a procrastinator if . . .

- You always find yourself rushing to get a project done at the last minute, no matter how much time you have to work on it.
- You have a cupboard full of supplies for new hobbies or craft projects you never got around to starting.
- You feel overwhelmed by the pressures placed on you as a woman, and the way you cope with the overwhelm is to keep yourself distracted.
- Your home is never tidier than when you have a major deadline looming.
- You feel guilt or shame when you take time out for yourself or pursue hobbies that don't have a "productive" purpose.
- You often find yourself volunteering to help out at your child's school or

run errands for loved ones, as being busy gives you a legitimate excuse to procrastinate on your dreams.

- You've had the same few tasks on your to-do list for months because they keep getting pushed to the following week.

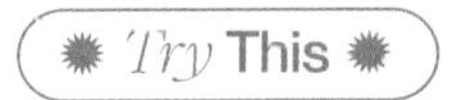

Review the descriptions of the different productivity archetypes once more and use the following questions to help you identify the archetype you most closely align with. You might like to journal on these questions or discuss them with friends to dive a little deeper.

- Think of the five people you are closest to in your life and consider which archetype you think each of them aligns with. What are the particular strengths you notice in them and which challenges do you think they face?
- Consider which of the productivity archetypes you find it most difficult to work with. Why do you think this is?
- Which productivity archetype did you resonate most with as you read the descriptions?
- Has reading the descriptions of the productivity archetypes helped make sense of anything for you?
- Were there any parts of the description you didn't align with?
- Do you find that you align with different archetypes in different areas of your life? For example, I'm very much a doer when it comes to work but more of a procrastinator in my personal life.
- Do you find that you embody different archetypes in different relationships or dynamics? For example, do you feel pressure to be a "perfect" daughter or mother?
- How does the archetype you identify most strongly with impact your relationship with productivity?

It might also be interesting to explore how the archetypes you don't identify with influence your relationship with productivity. For example, as a doer, I often feel a sense of shame when I cut corners in my rush to get things done, which makes me uncomfortable when working alongside a perfectionist who has a greater capacity for detail.

If you'd like a little more help identifying your productivity archetype, I have a free quiz that you can take on my website. You can find it at: www.sophiecliff.com/the-hustle-cure-quiz.

Knowing and understanding which productivity archetype (or archetypes) you most align with can be a huge help in untangling and redefining your relationship with productivity, success, and joy. It's important to note that these archetypes relate to your preferences—how you find it easiest to show up in the world—and are not fixed or unmoveable traits. There is also inherently some crossover between the archetypes—for example, perfectionists might be likely to procrastinate, and procrastinators might find themselves stuck dreaming. You might find that the stage of life you're in impacts your archetype—for example, as the mum of a toddler who runs her own business while writing a book, I find it much easier to fall into the doer category right now, whereas at other points in my life I have been more of a perfectionist.

How you choose to use your productivity archetype throughout the rest of the book is up to you. You may choose to read only the recommendations given for the archetype you most align with, or you might want to read everything, building your own menu of tips and ideas that feel good to you. Either way, I hope that they will be a positive force for you as you relinquish the hustle and embrace a life on your own terms.

LET'S RECAP

- There are four productivity archetypes that shape how we approach our goals and ambitions:
  - **DOERS:** Individuals driven by achievement who always seem to be busy.
  - **PERFECTIONISTS:** Those who hold themselves to the highest standards and are motivated by doing everything right.
  - **DREAMERS:** People who easily envision a better world but may struggle to turn their dreams into a reality.
  - **PROCRASTINATORS:** Those who are often highly creative but feel a bit lost and find it hard to take action.
- Productivity archetypes are not specific prescriptions but rather guideposts to help you better understand your relationship with productivity, success, and joy.
- Each archetype has its own unique strengths and challenges.
- The productivity archetype you most identify with may be impacted by your experiences or the unique pressures you face as a woman.

CHAPTER 3:

DEFINE SUCCESS ON YOUR OWN TERMS

When you were little, what did you want to be when you grew up? A teacher? A vet? A doctor? An astronaut? Unlike most children, I never really had a clear answer to that question. All I knew was that when I was an adult, I wanted to work in an office. In fact, I didn't just want to work in an office; I wanted to have my own office.

I can't recall how this dream of mine originated. It could have been the movies I watched, in which powerful, important women strutted around in heels and gazed out over the New York skyline from their corner offices. I'm almost certain that I was heavily influenced by a trip to the office my mum worked in, where I was captivated by the glamour of a stationery cupboard and the way her colleagues had decorated their desks and private offices with trinkets from home. Wherever the idea had come from, I was convinced that I'd know I'd achieved success if I had my own office. Even as I headed to university and transitioned from childhood to adulthood, my goal remained unchanged.

In January 2022, I found myself in possession of that office I'd long dreamt of. After a challenging decade spent building a corporate career working for huge global organisations like The Walt Disney Company and Hallmark, I left it all behind in 2019, retraining as a coach and starting my own business. My motivation to make a change was grounded in a desire to find more joy and freedom in my career, but I'll admit that the first few years were difficult—not only was there a global pandemic making things harder, but also the groundwork required to build a client base from scratch challenged me daily. By the start of 2022, however, it felt like I had some real momentum behind me. My coaching practice was at capacity, I was writing my first book, my group programmes were selling out, and I'd just won contracts to deliver well-being training to some impressive organisations. Most importantly, the growth of my business had made it possible to finally achieve that dream I had held since I was a little girl. I had my very own office, a space all to myself, nestled in the heart of the city centre, overlooking a beautiful park.

On paper, I was experiencing great success. My business revenue was growing rapidly, my calendar was full, and the opportunities just seemed to keep flowing my way. I felt like that woman I'd watched in the movies growing up—running from one meeting to the next, grabbing lunch on the go, working late in the office that I'd adorned with inspiring prints and expensive candles. But I didn't feel successful. I felt tired. Overwhelmed. Anxious that I was going to drop something and let someone down. I was working on weekends, something I'd always sworn I'd never do again when I had left corporate life, and I felt like a fraud—here I was telling everyone to choose joy, when I was struggling to prioritise it in my own life amidst the chaos of my hectic workload.

Thankfully, my training and experience as a positive psychologist helped me recognise what was happening before things got too bad. I've done enough work identifying my core values and defining my own version of success to notice when I'm chasing something that doesn't feel quite right for me, and I quickly realised that piling on extra work didn't feel good at all. What struck me from that experience was how easy it is to get caught up in the idea that busyness equals success, how tempting it is to say yes to every project, even when I have done all that work. It shouldn't come as a surprise though, because as we discussed in Chapter One, we live in a world that treats busyness and success—and, ultimately, happiness—as synonymous. That means that it's all too easy to couple our productivity with our self-worth.

We grow up believing that the more we get done, the more successful we'll be, and we're also reminded time and again that success is the pinnacle, the thing we should all be striving for. Don't believe me? Take a moment to think about the women who are most lauded and celebrated in our society. The ones who are interviewed in magazines and on podcasts, the ones whom we put on lists like the *Forbes* 30 Under 30 or applaud for managing to juggle it all. They're the women who seem to be racing through life, ticking off achievements, always working on a new project or developing a new skill. They're the ones who seem to be able to juggle their careers and family lives seamlessly, looking perfect while doing it. They're the women who, externally at least, fit the mould of "having it all." We equate voracious productivity with success, and we hold up the most productive people as our icons. It's little wonder that so many of us fall into the trap of thinking that success, and therefore happiness, lies on the other side of the next project or goal. It's little wonder that so many of us are running ourselves into the ground, burning ourselves out while trying to keep up with a myriad of expectations and pressures.

These pressures to get it all done, and quickly, impact everybody, but they are even greater for women. I've seen this play out with friends and clients. Our biological clocks play a role—if we know we want to have children, there can be a greater pressure to achieve traditional success in our careers throughout our twenties so that we have a solid safety net underneath us when we decide to start a family. And even if having children isn't on your agenda, you might still be impacted by the so-called motherhood penalty. One study found that women are identified as risky to employ because of their potential for future motherhood (Peterson Gloor, Okimoto, and King 2021). Ageing plays a role too. For example, a 2023 survey (Choi-Allum) found that over two-thirds of female workers age forty and older had experienced age discrimination at work, while our male counterparts were deemed to become wiser and more knowledgeable the older they got. Is it any wonder that we get swept up in trying to reach society's pinnacle of success before it's "too late"?

But if we pause and truly reflect, I think most of us would agree that chasing this version of success—the version that requires us to do more, be more, have more; the version that leaves no room for our humanness and our desires; the version that has a negative impact on our well-being—isn't serving us. It isn't making us any happier. In fact, it's often doing the opposite: leaving us with a dent in our self-worth and a constant fear that we're being left behind.

It's exhausting to try to hold ourselves to standards that we played no part in defining. I think it's time for us to start redefining success on our own terms.

Redefine the Idea of Success

In 2019, palliative care worker Bronnie Ware published her memoir, *The Top Five Regrets of the Dying*. In it, she shared her experience of working with dying people and the lessons she learnt from caring for them, in the hope that we might be able to learn how to live better from those who have gone before us. The top two regrets she lists in her book are as follows:

1. I wish I'd had the courage to live a life true to myself, not the life others expected of me.
2. I wish I hadn't worked so hard.

Out of all the people Bronnie Ware cared for over many years, these two regrets were the ones that came up most frequently. Isn't that powerful?

I think there are two key takeaways here when it comes to redefining the idea of success. First, it is crucial to define success on our own terms. We are all unique individuals with varying priorities and values, and we all have things we want to savour in our lives. What you care about and value will be different from what is most important to me, and that's okay—as long as we acknowledge that. The only way we are ever going to feel truly successful is if we live a life that feels authentic to us, and a big part of that is being intentional in figuring out what we actually want, instead of simply getting caught up in the expectations and milestones set out for us by society or our communities.

Second, our definition of success needs to encompass more than just work because life is about more than just our careers. That might sound obvious, but how many times have you given up on a personal goal because of a pressing work deadline or skipped a dinner with friends because a project needed to be completed? Work can form a significant part of our identities, and it's easy for pressure from our bosses or comparison to our peers to further inflate the importance of our careers. However, we must be able to zoom out a little and give work an appropriate amount of focus in our lives if we're going to avoid the regrets listed above. When we prioritise work above everything else, what are we missing out on? When we value ourselves simply by our earnings or our career achievements, how does that impact our self-worth?

What I took away from Ware's book is this: we have been gifted one precious and beautiful life, and we have to make the most of it. To do that, we must be intentional in figuring out what we want out of life, instead of letting life take us along for the ride. Even if we're lucky enough to live well into our nineties, our time here is fleeting. And yet so many of us find ourselves cruising through it on autopilot as we pile on the pressure and expect ourselves to cram even more in. And what's it all for? We know from Chapter One and our exploration of arrival fallacy that stacking up the achievements doesn't bring us more happiness. In fact, one of the biggest studies in positive psychology, involving almost a million people, suggests that it might be the other way around, with happiness and other positive emotions preceding successful outcomes (Lyubomirsky, King, and Diener 2005).

The reason why experiencing positive emotions can increase our chances of success can be explained by the broaden-and-build theory, developed by prominent social psychologist Barbara Fredrickson (2004). She theorised that while negative emotions can prompt us to adopt narrow, survival-oriented behaviours, such as engaging our fight, flight, or freeze responses, positive emotions broaden our awareness and encourage new thoughts and actions.

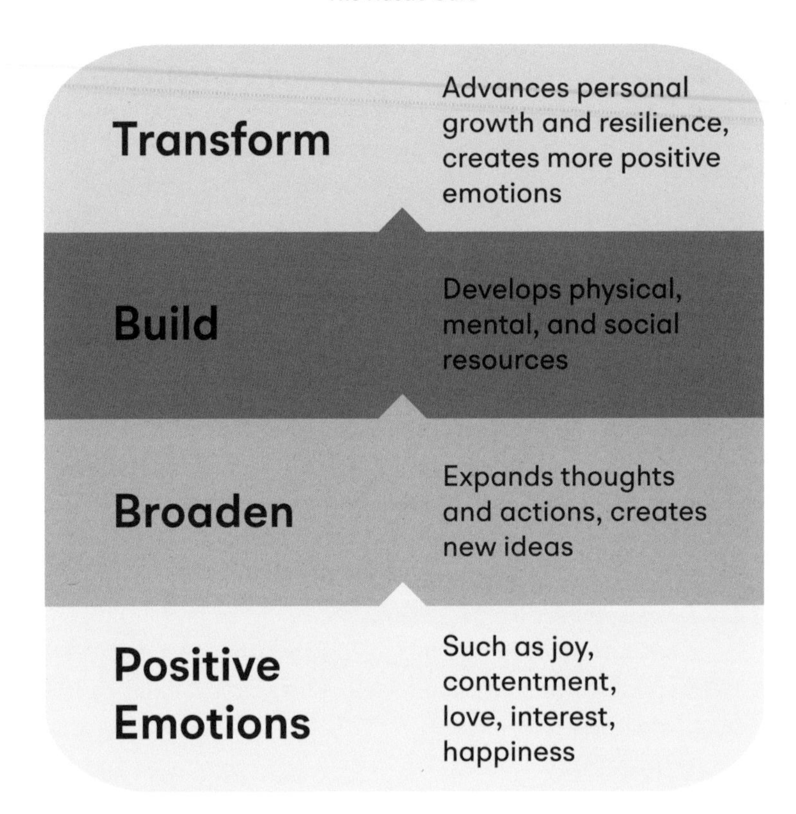

As illustrated in the diagram above, the idea is that when we experience positive emotions, we expand our thinking and create new ideas. We are then able to build new mental, physical, and social resources that help us advance our personal growth and resilience, leading to a positive transformation. Here's an example: if you arrive at a work conference feeling good, you might be more likely to introduce yourself to someone new. You strike up an engaging conversation with them and keep in touch after the event. When the time comes for you to look for a new job, they might be able to introduce you to someone in their network or give you advice that helps you nail the interview. But perhaps more importantly, you've formed a new connection and experienced the joy that comes with getting to know someone, broadening your horizons.

If we were to pause and consider what we truly want out of life, many of us might realise that the traditional measure of success we've been chasing—the one that requires us to pursue bigger, better, more—might not be serving us in the way we'd hoped. In fact, it might be the very thing keeping us feeling trapped in a cycle of burnout and self-doubt.

Maybe it's time to redefine the idea of success, and I know just the place to start.

What If Joy Were Our Measure of Success?

Given that I go by the moniker of the Joyful Coach, it might not be all that surprising that I'm suggesting that joy is a better measure of success than simply what we achieve. But when we read those regrets from Ware's book and remember that life is more fleeting than any of us care to admit, it's hard to believe that anything else is as important as the amount of joy we feel in each and every day. That has certainly been my experience. Following a traumatic bereavement in 2016, my measure of success shifted dramatically. Prior to that experience, I'd been interested in all the ego-based stuff—money, status, achievements, accolades. I achieved a lot of it too, but it never made me happy. When the universe served me a very real and difficult reminder that life is not a dress rehearsal, I understood why: Because it wasn't the stuff that added meaning or purpose to my life. It wasn't the stuff that I was going to care about at the end of my life. And yet I had let it absorb so much of my limited time and energy. It was that experience that led me to first consider joy as a measure of success, and I've been encouraging others to do the same ever since.

There are a few things I want to clarify before we explore how we can use joy as a measure of success. Firstly, what do I mean by *joy*? It's a term than can be hard to define, and many confuse it with happiness, but research suggests that they are two different concepts. Happiness is often circumstantial—for example, we might feel happy when it's our birthday or when someone gives us positive feedback. Joy, on the other hand, is something that we can cultivate, and we can experience it even when the giddy high of happiness feels out of reach. It can also be experienced in conjunction with more challenging emotions, such as grief or stress. Joy tends to emerge when we're feeling present and in the moment. Connection and gratitude are big predictors of joy—when we feel part of a bigger community and thankful for all that we have in our lives, joy tends to flow.

Secondly, when I talk about joyful living, I'm not suggesting that we should feel joyful 24/7. I don't believe that experiencing joy around the clock is a possible or reasonable expectation to set for ourselves. In fact, part of the reason joy feels so good is because we've experienced contrasting emotions. I also don't believe that we have to eliminate all the challenging stuff in our lives in order to feel joy. Instead, I believe that joyful living is about giving the good stuff in our lives as much attention as we do the bad stuff and creating room to be as present as possible for all that good stuff.

In my experience of supporting clients over the last five or six years, I have seen that women in particular find it challenging to prioritise joy and to keep it front and centre in their own definition of success. They may not even know what would add more joy to their lives. That's unsurprising given that as a society, we celebrate women for their selflessness and ability to always put others' needs above their own. We have been conditioned to believe that joy is the reward for being a "good" woman, that we have to earn our happiness by "having it all." But that is no way to live. In the words of Mary Oliver, "Joy is not made to be a crumb." It is an essential, vital, life-giving emotion that we deserve to experience as regularly as possible. And if you're still worried that prioritising your own joy will make you selfish, remember that you are a model to those around you. If you want your children or loved ones to prioritise joy in their lives, you need to start modelling that it is safe to do so.

With that in mind, let's work through a little exercise.

If joy were your only measure of success, how successful would your life feel right now? That can feel like a daunting question, so let me help you break it down. Give each of the categories below a score out of ten based on how joyful they feel to you right now, with ten being as joyful as you can imagine and one being completely lacking in joy. Try not to overthink this and instead jot down the first number that comes to mind:

- Friends and family = /10
- Work and career = /10
- Romantic relationship = /10
- Health and fitness = /10
- Fun and leisure = /10
- Personal growth = /10

Once you've given each area of your life a score for how joyful it feels, take a step back and reflect. Are you surprised? Do your scores feel consistent across the board, or is there variation? Do you have any ideas about why that might be?

Remember that, as women, we often face unique pressures and expectations in each of these areas of life. Society may tell us that we need to be the perfect mother, wife, employee, and friend, all while maintaining a healthy work-life balance full of carefree leisure and fun. Trying to adhere to these unrealistic standards can make it challenging to find joy and feel truly successful, even when we're excelling by traditional measures.

Given your scores, how successful does your life feel now? Go gently here—I know that when I completed this exercise years ago, it felt quite overwhelming to realise that in the pursuit of traditional success, I'd been sacrificing the things that were most important to me. I held a lot of regret and guilt about the experiences and moments I'd missed out on. If you're feeling the same way, be kind to yourself and trust that we'll look at the changes that can help you throughout the rest of this book.

The Freedom of Knowing What Is Enough

Before we get on to writing your own definition of success, there's one more idea I want to explore. What would having enough look like for you?

Enough is not a sexy word. Not in a society that celebrates indulgence, opulence, and abundance. Enough can feel basic, boring, miserly even—and, let's face it, not that joyful. But would you believe me if I told you that learning to recognise what enough looks like for me has been one of the most freeing mindset shifts I've experienced?

As women, we often operate from a place of scarcity. Maybe it's because we've been conditioned to believe that our worth is tied to our appearance, our relationships, and our professional achievements. Maybe it's because we've grown up in a world where the gender pay gap persists and we feel like we always need to be striving for more to prove our value. For me, I consider my own working-class family roots coming in to play—a hereditary survival instinct that reminds me to never rest on my laurels. I also recall graduating into a recession, when there were quite literally not enough jobs to go around. Wherever that conditioning comes from, I can see now that a scarcity mindset doesn't serve us. It pulls us away from our intuition and core values and convinces us that we need more in order to be happy and content. Asking ourselves what enough looks like is the most effective way I've found of overriding that constant, draining drive for more.

Because when I really sit and ponder my answers to that question, I realise that I need a lot less than I've always believed. For me, having enough looks like a job that fulfils and challenges me, doing work that allows me to make a positive impact in the world. It's having a home that can house our little family, with enough space to entertain friends and have the people we love come to stay. It's having plenty of time and space to create, to get outdoors, and to live life in the moment. It's having enough money to sustain my and my husband's creative pursuits, with a little bit left over for living. And that's it. I don't need a fancy job title. I don't need a house with more bedrooms than we'll ever use. I don't need a huge salary, or a flashy car, or a wardrobe bursting with designer purchases. I don't need five-star luxury holidays, endless shopping hauls, or a postcode in the very best area of town. I don't need to look like a supermodel.

And it's in realising this that the freedom comes. Because if I don't need those things, if I can live a really good life without them, I can free myself from the endless hustle required to achieve them. I can stop damaging my self-worth by trying to achieve things that won't add any more happiness to my life. I can recognise that I already have enough and focus my efforts on truly appreciating those things and the joy they bring. I don't need to race to acquire wealth so that I can retire early, because I can enjoy life right here, right now.

Your definition of enough might look different from mine. That's okay. The key is actually figuring out what enough looks and feels like for you and letting that be your North Star. In the world we live in, choosing to seek only what feels like enough instead of getting swept up in the endless pursuit of more is a radical act, one that has the potential to transform how we care for one another and this planet we live on. It is also one of the most freeing things you can do for yourself.

Because choosing enough isn't boring. It's freedom. Freedom from the goals and ambitions that no longer serve you. Freedom to pour your energy into the things that you truly care about. Freedom from the need to earn more, have more, be more. Freedom to be who you are and to embrace all your uniqueness. And most of all, freedom to enjoy life in all its imperfect and beautiful glory.

This isn't about letting go of your ambitions or settling for less. It's simply about choosing the ambitions that are right for you and letting go of the hold that everything else might have on you. When we do that, we know that we're achieving true productivity by only pouring our energy into the pursuits that will add value and joy to our lives.

One of the biggest obstacles to figuring out what enough looks like to you is blocking out the noise and influences that surround you. It can be hard to focus on our own inner voice and desires when we are constantly being bombarded with advertisements and other people's opinions, but there are a few practical things we can do to turn down the volume. Here are some ideas:

- Have a digital detox. Unfollow any social media accounts that make you feel less than or drive you to want to purchase more or look differently. Be mindful as you scroll, noticing how you feel when you land on certain posts or accounts, and be liberal with your unfollows. It's amazing how quickly your internal narrative can shift when you're not comparing your life to those of strangers on the internet.
- Recognise who in your life adds to the pressure you're feeling. Do your parents or colleagues freely share their opinions on your choices, for example, or do you feel a pressure to keep up with friends? While you can't remove these influences as easily as you can accounts on social media, simply being aware of the impact they're having on you can help you be more mindful when seeking advice or guidance.
- Consider who benefits from you chasing certain goals. For example, when I realised that my poor body image was helping weight loss and beauty companies make a serious amount of money, it became easier to realise that the beauty ideal is a myth created to sell us stuff, which lessened its power over me. Perhaps you might realise that the pressure to be a "perfect" mother helps market certain products, or maybe you'll become aware that our constant drive for more keeps us distracted from the real social issues that impact our lives.
- Ask yourself: Would I still want this if I couldn't tell anybody about it? This question is great for helping you clarify which goals or endeavours add value to your life and which you may be pursuing in an effort to keep up or please other people.

LET IT GO

With all this in mind, are there any measures of success that you would actively like to reject? When we let go of the ambitions or milestones that don't feel right to us, we create more space to focus on the ones that do.

For example, maybe you've realised you don't actually want to climb the corporate ladder and would prefer to pursue a career that allows for a work-life balance and more flexibility. Or perhaps, like my client Elise, you've discovered that the pressure to have it all—the perfect family, the successful career, and the enviable lifestyle—is less important to you than you might have first thought, and you'd feel happier pouring your energy into personal growth and experiences. When I did this exercise with my client Li, she realised that she had been working towards a version of success that had been heavily influenced by her immigrant parents and the hopes they had for her. As difficult as it was to uncouple her self-worth from their expectations of her, doing so enabled her to make changes that felt more joyful and fulfilling to her.

What could be possible for you if you stopped busying yourself with things you don't even want? Many of us pursue goals that don't align with our true desires when we listen to our culture's pressures instead of our own goals. But by rejecting these external measures of success, we can create space for what truly matters to us.

Defining Success Your Way

Okay, so now it's time to create a definition of success that feels true to you. Does that idea make you feel excited and hopeful or a little bit intimidated? It probably depends on the archetype you most identified with in Chapter Two.

The Doer

If you identify as a doer, you might never have given your definition of success much consideration. Women who are doers tend to be so focused on getting the next thing ticked off the list that it's rare for them to stop and reflect on what it's all for. This was certainly the case for my client Maria. Maria jumped straight from her law degree into a competitive firm and spent the first two decades of her career climbing the ranks and sacrificing everything else in her life to make partner. But when she finally did, she didn't feel the overwhelming surge of success she was expecting—instead, she felt exhausted and burnt out. She ended up being signed off work for three months to recover.

We can't trust that achieving the version of success that society has laid out for us will make us happy. Instead, we need to consider how we want to feel and what is most important to us. When we do that, we can ensure that all the energy we're pouring into doing is moving us closer to the place we want to be—a place that feels more fulfilling, purposeful, and joyful. The exercise at the end of this chapter will help you get clear on your own version of success. It might feel tricky if it's not something you've ever considered before, but I'm pretty sure that it will bring up some important revelations too.

The Perfectionist

If you're more of a perfectionist, you might find the idea of carving out your own definition of success intimidating and overwhelming. Women who are perfectionists prefer to follow the rules, and so turning your back on the traditional measures of success might feel uncomfortable. But it's key that you do so if you want to experience more joy and contentment in your life.

Pay close attention to how other people's opinions or perceptions might be shaping your definition of success. For example, my client Li was always motivated by being the "perfect" daughter and achieving the ambitions that her parents had for her. This led Li to pursue a career she didn't find fulfilling, and she felt like she'd missed out on other things that were important to her, such as travelling, in pursuit of these goals. Realising that being "perfect" for someone else was never going to make her happy empowered Li to do the challenging work of shaking off those external definitions of success and start getting in touch with what it was she really wanted.

As hard as it might be, try to hold off on worrying too much about how you'll achieve your definition of success at this time—we'll figure that out in later chapters.

The Dreamer

If you identify as a dreamer, defining your own version of success will probably come quite naturally to you, given your creativity and talent for imagining a better way of doing things. However, as my client Samia found, sharing big ideas as women often opens us up to resistance or scepticism. When she shared her vision for a new networking space that would bring women from different communities together, she was all but laughed at by her male peers, who encouraged her to focus more on her day job. Four years and plenty of incredible networking events in, it's Samia who's laughing. If you've experienced similar resistance or ridicule, don't let it hold you back—your unique perspective and vision are valuable and deserve to be explored.

As you explore what success looks like to you, consider capturing some of your ideas in a vision board, either made the old-fashioned way, with cutouts from magazines, or created online by using a tool like Canva or sourcing images from Pinterest and other online platforms. While creating your vision board, notice what it is that you're most drawn to and what it is about those things that most excites you.

It might also be useful to try to jot down any specific details that come to mind at this stage. The clearer you can be on what your definition of success entails, the easier it will be to create your plan of action in later chapters. If we leave it too vague, it can be tempting to stay in the dreaming stage instead of taking the steps that will make it a reality!

The Procrastinator

Finally, if you're a procrastinator, you might experience some resistance when it comes to defining your own version of success. Maybe you feel burnt by having done an exercise like this before and you're struggling to take action to make it a reality. Or perhaps, deep down, you don't feel as though your own vision for success is realistic. Maybe you fear failure, along with what trying and failing would mean for your sense of self-worth. But perhaps you also fear success—and what achieving everything you desire would mean for your identity.

This was the case for my client Jade. Jade spent the first part of her career working as a speech therapist, a job that earned her lots of praise and respect within her community. But while she enjoyed elements of her job, aspects of her role compromised her well-being and fulfilment, and she found herself burning out regularly. Jade harboured a dream to retrain as a florist, but she struggled to even let herself admit it was something she wanted. She suspected that, in making a change, she would lose the respect and praise that came with her current career.

As women, we can find it challenging to pursue our true passions and desires when we worry about what others will think or when we feel guilty for putting our own needs first. Acknowledging those fears and pushing through them allowed Jade to start defining success on her own terms and taking action to achieve it. The same can be true for you. Get clear on what sits behind your procrastination, and you might find that clarity lessens the power it holds over you.

DO IT YOUR WAY

It's time to define your own version of success. To help you do that, I want to share a tool from positive psychology called the Best Possible Self exercise. This exercise, which was developed in 2001 by Dr. Laura King, has been shown to boost hope, improve our well-being, and increase optimism. But, most importantly for us, it has also been shown to help people find more clarity about their goals and ambitions.

The exercise is a hybrid visualisation and journaling exercise. Here are the instructions:

Think about your life in the future. Imagine that everything has gone as well as it possibly could. You have worked hard and succeeded at accomplishing all of your life goals. Think of this as the realisation of all of your life dreams. Now, write about what you imagined.

The instructions from the original study invited participants to write about what they had imagined for twenty minutes, then to repeat the exercise on four consecutive days. However, evidence suggests that the exercise is useful even if completed only once or twice.

Once you've completed the exercise, take some time to reflect on what you visualised and wrote about. What was most important to you in your vision? Has reflecting on the prompt changed how you think about success at all?

Here are some tips to help you get the most from this exercise:

- Don't worry too much if you find it difficult the first time you reflect on this prompt. If you've never spent much time considering your own definition of success, you might find yourself drawing a blank. That's okay—just keep revisiting the exercise until your vision starts to flow.
- Set yourself a specific time frame. For example, consider what you want life to look like in five or ten years' time.
- Remember to take a holistic approach, thinking about your whole life and not just your career, finances, or social status.
- Think about how you can keep your future vision front of mind. One way of doing this might be to create a vision board on

Pinterest, with images and quotes that reflect how you hope the future to look and feel.

- Make an evening of it with friends. Gather your best pals, take some time to reflect on the prompt individually, then talk through what you each imagined. I find that, sometimes, it's easier for people to clarify their vision by talking it through rather than only writing about it.
- Consider revisiting this exercise on a regular basis. I like to complete it every three or four months. Doing so allows me to stay connected with my own definition of success, and it also gives me the opportunity to tweak it if I feel called to.

LET'S RECAP

- We live in a society that equates achievement with success, but exploring the most common regrets shows us that there is a need to define success on our own terms, especially as women who often face unique pressures and expectations.
- Pursuing a version of success that doesn't feel true to us can be detrimental to our self-worth and can contribute to exhaustion and burnout.
- Joy can be a more meaningful measure of success than achievement, particularly for those of us who feel the pressure to have it all.
- Knowing what enough looks like can help us create more freedom in our lives and let go of the endless pursuit of more that can leave us feeling overwhelmed and unfulfilled.
- Defining success on our own terms is key in helping us focus our limited energies and resources on what truly matters to us.

CHAPTER 4:

GET THE REST YOU NEED TO THRIVE

Remember when the pandemic first hit and we had that sweeping realisation that we'd be spending more time at home due to lockdown? Did you set yourself a goal for what you wanted to use that time for? I remember that social media was awash with people learning how to knit for the first time or vowing to get fitter than ever. Others downloaded Duolingo in a bid to learn a new language, and many had the same idea as my husband and committed to using the time to master some new recipes.

I set myself the goal of resting. Amidst all the panic and confusion of the early days of the pandemic, the silver lining I arrived at was that maybe I'd finally be able to address the tiredness I couldn't seem to shake. The year preceding the first lockdown had been a hectic one for me. I'd completed my coaching qualification, set up my business, turned thirty, and quit my corporate career. All the late nights and weekends spent working away, combined with the adrenaline of making a significant life pivot, had left me feeling exhausted, and I was determined to use the enforced social isolation to finally catch up on sleep.

And catch up on sleep I did! No commutes, dinner dates, or late-night parties meant I was able to get to bed early and sleep later than usual, averaging about nine or ten hours a night. Yet I still felt tired. At first, I thought it must have been because of all the stress and uncertainty accompanying that time. Sure, I was sleeping more than usual, but I was also worrying a lot too, and I chalked the exhaustion up to that. But then I stumbled across a TEDx Talk that made me realise there was much more at play.

In that 2019 TEDx Talk, physician and award-winning author Dr. Saundra Dalton-Smith discusses how, in order to feel well rested, we need more than just sleep. In fact, she argues that we need to ensure we're getting seven different types of rest—physical rest (sleep and naps, for example), mental rest, spiritual rest, sensory rest, emotional rest, creative rest, and social rest. Watching that TEDx Talk was revelatory for me because, for the first time, I realised that rest is about more than physically recharging.

Up until that point, I'd believed that to ensure I had enough energy to achieve my goals and be as productive as I'd like to be, I simply needed to focus on getting enough sleep. But suddenly, I could see that recharging is about so much more than physical recovery—it's also about ensuring we have the emotional, mental, creative, and spiritual resources we require to pursue our ambitions. This is especially true for women, who often face unique responsibilities—such as bearing children, maintaining social connections, and managing the mental load, in addition to everything else—that can leave them feeling depleted in multiple areas of their lives.

As often happens when I have this sort of lightbulb moment, I became obsessed with exploring this topic in more detail. I read everything I could get my hands on, observed how my clients talked about rest in our coaching sessions, and discussed the topic for hours with my friends and peers. This exploration led me to develop my own rest-and-recharge model:

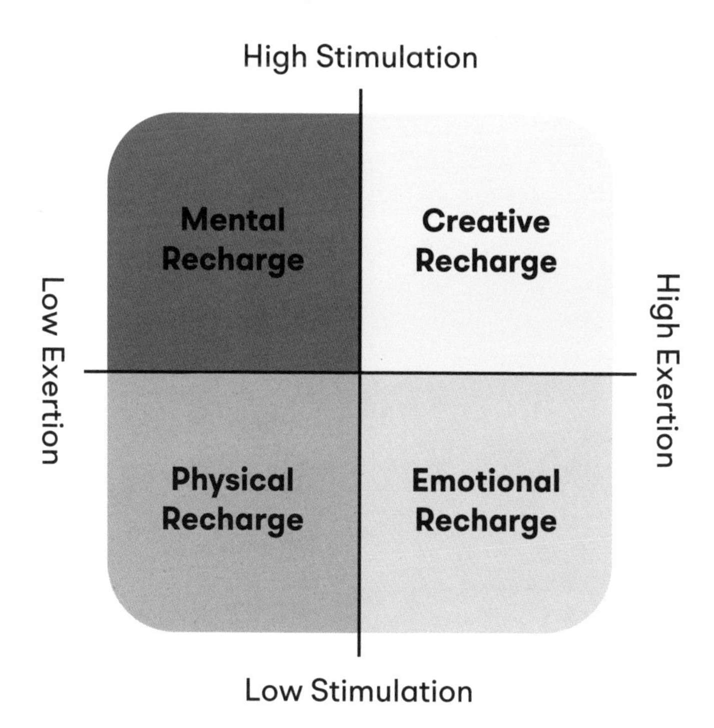

Prior to developing this model, I had assumed that rest was all about the activities in the bottom left quadrant—things that were both low stimulation and low exertion, such as getting a massage, sleeping, and napping. However, I came to understand that if we are to feel truly recharged, we need to ensure we're prioritising activities in all four quadrants. This gives us the opportunity to not just recharge our physical energy but also our mental, creative, and emotional energies too.

For example, walking in the woods (a practice known as forest bathing or *shinrin-yoku*) can be incredibly restful even though it requires physical movement, as it lowers cortisol levels and provides a calming sensory experience. On the other hand, scrolling through social media, while low in physical exertion, can be mentally and emotionally taxing, making it less restful to your system. You may have noticed that hanging out with friends lifts your spirits and helps you recharge from a day at work that has required a lot of mental exertion and that a good yoga session can help you emotionally rest if you've been under a high amount of stress.

I'll explain more about why focusing on each of these four quadrants is important later in the chapter, particularly in the context of the unique challenges and pressures we face. But for now I want to address a question that might be on your mind: What does rest have to do with productivity, and why is it especially crucial for women to prioritise?

What Does Rest Have to Do with Productivity?

In the coming chapters, I'm going to share more about how you can harness your unique strengths and resources to get more done in a way that works for you. I'm a big believer that we all need different things to master our productivity groove, and the whole premise of this book is about helping you build your own personalised plan. However, there's one thing that we can all benefit from more of, and that's rest. I want to dedicate a whole chapter to resting and recharging because, often, in the rush to get more and more done, it's the first thing we sacrifice, and it can have a detrimental impact on our ability to take further action.

I've certainly been guilty of sacrificing rest in the past. Whenever I had an assignment due at university, you could find me in the library tapping away on my laptop long after midnight. As my roles and responsibilities grew in my corporate jobs, the trains I'd catch into work would get earlier and earlier, and eventually my alarm would go off well before dawn. And when I first started building my coaching business around my full-time job, I filled every available moment of rest with studying for my qualification or trying to get my website set up. I know I'm not the only one—most of my coaching clients come to me burnt out from trying to squeeze as much as they can into every margin of life, saying yes to every commitment and never giving themselves the time they need to fully rest and recuperate.

Sometimes, it can feel as though sacrificing rest is the only way to keep up. When it feels like we've got too much to get done in the hours available to us, cutting into our rest and leisure time seems like a logical thing to do—and many of us are indeed doing just that: data collected over the past decade shows that women in the UK and the US spend around 14 percent less time on leisure pursuits each day than men (OECD 2021). Many of us feel guilty for taking time for ourselves, believing that we should always prioritise the needs of others—or of our career, our appearance, or our personal development. But this constant self-sacrifice too often leads to burnout and resentment, and ultimately a decrease in our well-being and productivity.

Studies suggest that taking a break to focus on recharging is the key for productivity. For example, research from the International Foundation of Employee Benefit Plans conducted in 2023 found that using annual leave improved employee productivity by up to 40 percent and reduced the risk of sick leave by 28 percent.

When we take the time to rest and recharge, we give ourselves a better chance of performing well by reducing stress, enhancing our memory, increasing creativity, and improving our overall cognitive functioning. Studies from Durham University (2016) have also shown that our ability to take rest is linked to our well-being, something that we need to be more mindful of as women, given that we are 40 percent more likely to suffer from insomnia than men (Mallampalli and Carter 2014). Simply put, when we aren't getting adequate downtime, not only do we put ourselves on a path to burnout, but we also risk jeopardising the quality of our output. And of course, let's not forget that when we are exhausted, it's much harder to find joy and live a fulfilling life that feels aligned with our authentic definition of success.

This is something I used to experience a lot in my previous career. I remember working with my team on a big retail marketing campaign. The organisation had invested millions of pounds into landing a significant activation in several high-street stores, and I was responsible for coordinating multiple departments to ensure everything landed as we hoped. I worked on the project for months, managing critical paths, attending weekly meetings, and ensuring the communication between different teams was clear and concise. I managed the project on top of an already-full workload, never communicating to my boss that I might need some extra support, and I neglected to take any annual leave for the three months we were planning the campaign. I played the part of having and being able to do it all, desperate not to appear weak or uncapable, but the truth is that it was too much for me to handle on top of my other roles and responsibilities. By the time our activation landed in stores, I had fallen ill with a throat infection that meant I missed the big launch day. My desire to be productive had left me with nothing in the tank, and eventually, my body gave up.

When we set off on a long journey in the car, the first thing we do is ensure we have enough fuel in the tank to get us to our destination. We need to start thinking about our own energy in the same way, ensuring we're keeping the levels high enough to meet the expectations we place on ourselves, and the way we do that is by getting enough rest. So, what restful activities fill your energy tank? And how can you ensure you get enough of them?

Knowing when you're most likely to sacrifice rest can help you create a plan for prioritising it, even when life gets busy. Take some time to consider when you've sacrificed rest in the past and what your triggers have been. Are there any insights you can use to help you in the future? Here are some ideas to consider:

- Whose needs are you most likely to prioritise before your own? For example, the needs of your children, your company, etc.
- When do you feel most keen to prove your capabilities? What triggers this desire to prove yourself? For example, do you feel like you have to overcompensate to make up for a lack of confidence at work?
- What habits do you sacrifice first when you become busy? Why do you think this is?
- What did you see modelled to you about rest by the women in your life when you were growing up? How do you think this has impacted how you prioritise rest?
- How has sacrificing rest in the past impacted your productivity?
- How has sacrificing rest in the past impacted the amount of joy you feel?

A Model to Help You Rest and Recharge

Now that we know why rest is important, particularly for women who often juggle multiple roles and responsibilities, I want to return to the rest-and-recharge model I shared with your earlier. As you can see from the model, there are four types of activities we need to engage in to fully recharge:

- **LOW EXERTION, LOW STIMULATION:** These types of activities help us physically recharge.
- **LOW EXERTION, HIGH STIMULATION:** These types of activities help us mentally recharge.
- **HIGH EXERTION, HIGH STIMULATION:** These types of activities help us creatively recharge.
- **HIGH EXERTION, LOW STIMULATION:** These types of activities help us emotionally recharge.

Let's look at each quadrant in turn.

Physical recharge

We'll start with the bottom left quadrant, which is all about the activities that help us physically recharge. These activities, which include things like sleeping, napping, getting a massage, or lying down to watch a comforting TV show, are perhaps the typical ones that spring to mind when we think of rest, and they are a vital part of ensuring we feel refreshed and recharged. Research has shown that not getting an inadequate amount of sleep significantly hampers workplace performance, with one study showing that insomnia is responsible for $63.2 billion of lost productivity every year in the US (Kessler 2011). Additionally, research has also shown that loss of sleep can activate anxiety in individuals who are high-risk for it (Goldstein et al. 2013), something that women need to be particularly mindful of given that they are significantly more likely than men to develop an anxiety disorder in their lifetime (McLean et al. 2011).

One thing to note here is that it's important that we keep stimulation low to physically recharge. It might feel relaxing to lie in bed scrolling TikTok or Instagram, but doing so will keep your mind stimulated, making it difficult for you to get the rest you need.

Here are some ideas to help you physically recharge:

- Make sure you're getting enough sleep for the season: research shows that we might need up to two hours more sleep each night in the winter months (Seidler et al. 2023). You might experiment with planning fewer evening activities during the winter to catch more rest.
- Set some communication boundaries. It's hard to get decent rest when our phones are pinging or lighting up next to us on the bedside tables, but we're so used to being connected that it can be hard to switch off completely. A few years ago, my mum established a great boundary, letting us know that if we need her urgently after eight p.m., we should call her landline. That way, she knows she is still contactable in an emergency, but her wind-down period isn't disrupted by constant notifications on her smartphone.
- Allow yourself to take a nap. Sleep scientists have shown that if you're not able to get enough sleep at night (fellow parents, I'm in that trench with you!), even a short nap can be effective in helping you recharge. It's likely that you will experience some resistance to taking a nap, especially if you have a lot on your to-do list, but when you consider the amount of time you spend scrolling on your phone each day, you can probably find twenty minutes to recharge your batteries.
- Treat yourself to a massage or spa day. This can be a great way to get some physical rest if you suffer from insomnia or other sleep disturbances. If money is tight, you could request vouchers or contributions as a birthday gift or perhaps consider other low-stimulation, low-exertion activities you can enjoy at home, such as taking a long bath.

Mental recharge

Moving in a clockwise direction, our next quadrant reveals that we can mentally recharge by engaging in activities that are still low in exertion but higher in stimulation. Put simply, they're things that don't require a huge amount of physical energy but stimulate your brain.

Activities that fall into this category include reading, journaling, catching up with friends, connecting with your purpose, and meditating. These activities contribute to making you feel more recharged by giving you time and space to process your daily life, your identity, and your goals. Research has shown that processing in this way is key for reducing stress and avoiding burnout, both of which can hamper our productivity. These activities can be particularly important for women who tend to carry more of the mental load and find it challenging to switch off from the running to-do list in their mind.

Ideas to help you mentally recharge:

- Experiment with using a meditation app, such as Headspace or Calm, to try out different meditations. If you struggle with these sorts of apps, why not book a meditation class with a friend? Accountability can be key to taking action when it comes to recharging.
- Try writing in the morning. The idea, taken from Julia Cameron's book *The Artist's Way* (2020), involves writing three stream-of-consciousness pages each morning, and it can be a great way to notice what's on your mind and begin to process it. If sitting down and writing for ten minutes feels unmanageable to you, why not experiment with recording voice notes on your drive to work, detailing how you're feeling that day?
- Read a book from a genre you wouldn't normally choose. Trying something new can be a more stimulating experience than reading an old favourite, meaning that it's more likely to help you explore different perspectives.
- Set up a regular date with friends. A few years ago, one of my good pals started a book club, and we meet every six weeks. It has been a powerful source of mental replenishment for me. Firstly, I find that I'm much less likely to flake if I've made a commitment to someone else, and secondly, being part of a book club has made it easier for me to carve out more time to read.

Creative recharge

Have you ever noticed that when you take a trip, you feel more energised, even if you're physically tired? I get this every time I visit New York City—I return home with aching feet from pounding block after block but full of ideas and energy to pour into my work. That's because I've been engaged in activities that are both high exertion and high stimulation. These sorts of activities help us recharge because they put creative fuel in our tanks, filling us up with new ideas, perspectives, and skills that we can use to work towards our goals.

Activities that fall into this category include going for a walk in nature, attending a creative class or workshop, travelling to a new place, visiting an exhibition, and attending a concert. Creatively recharging is important even if you don't have a job or goals that you would define as typically creative. We all need inspiration, and these sorts of activities help us find it.

Ideas to help you creatively recharge:

- Visit an art gallery or museum. A study by Cotter and Pawelski (2021) found that experiencing art this way can help improve our well-being and enhance human flourishing. Don't worry if you don't have a huge amount of knowledge about art or design; simply being in the environment will feel inspiring. Research what exhibitions are happening in your area, and give it a go. You might just love it!
- Go for an awe walk. An awe walk involves walking around your neighbourhood and trying to take in your surroundings as if you were seeing them for the first time, pausing to notice what inspires and uplifts you. If you're really pushed for time, you could even turn your commute into an awe journey, challenging yourself to take in a familiar route through fresh eyes.
- Challenge yourself to learn a new skill. You could take a class or simply find some videos on YouTube to help you—it's the act of focusing on a new task that holds the benefit, not the way you go about it. You could get your kids or friends involved for some extra accountability. Release the pressure to create something perfect, and embrace being a beginner.

Emotional recharge

The final quadrant centres on activities that are high exertion but low stimulation. These sorts of activities help our bodies and minds process the physical side effects of stress, which in turn helps us emotionally recharge and build greater resilience.

In their book *Burnout: Solve Your Stress Cycle*, Emily and Amelia Nagoski (2020) write that "physical activity is the single most efficient strategy for completing the stress response cycle," with the reason being that when we move our bodies, we signal to our brains that we have fought off whatever was causing us stress and that it's safe to relax. Given the increased pressures and stress that women face, it's important that we make the time to process it if we want to avoid burnout or other illnesses.

Activities that fall into this category include going for a run, dancing in your kitchen, having sex, attending a yoga class, and practising breath work. It's all about being in your body instead of your mind and increasing your tolerance for stress and other emotions in the process.

Ideas to help you emotionally recharge:

- Embrace your inner Taylor Swift and shake it off! Just a few minutes of shaking your arms and legs can be enough to help you start to emotionally self-regulate. I often like to do this in between coaching calls, as it helps me reset and reconnect with the present moment.
- Push yourself to go that little bit further. If you already regularly work out, see if you can push yourself for a few minutes more than you usually would. Notice how you feel as a result—when we can see the impact our efforts are having on our emotional health, we feel more motivated to keep it up.
- Explore the art of breath work. Deep breathing can downregulate your stress response, particularly if you're not experiencing a high level of stress. There are lots of videos on YouTube to help you get started.
- Ask for the help you need. Often, when I speak to women, they say they have a desire to move their bodies but struggle to find the time. If that resonates, I urge you to ask the people in your life for help in finding that time. Stress can have a debilitating impact on our physical and mental health, and even thirty minutes of gentle movement a week can go a long way in completing the stress cycle.

A Note on Other People

One last thing to consider when it comes to recharging is the role other people play in helping you feel energised—or not. Knowing whether you're an extrovert or an introvert can be very useful information to have. We've been led to believe that extroverts are loud and introverts are quiet, but that isn't always the case—the difference between the two is where they get their energy from. Extroverts recharge their energy by spending time with others, whereas introverts need time alone to feel fully refreshed.

For women, who often face societal expectations to be nurturing and accommodating, it can be especially challenging to honour our own needs when it comes to social interaction. We may feel guilty for saying no to social invitations or worry that we'll be perceived as selfish for prioritising alone time. Knowing which you identify as can help you choose the activities that will feel most energising to you—for example, if you're an extrovert, you might find that setting up a regular check-in with a friend helps you recharge, while introverts might prefer to be alone with their journal. Also, some people may identify differently in different settings. For example, they might get a lot of energy from working on a team in a professional setting but prefer to hang out alone on the weekends.

Another thing to consider when it comes to other people is that how they make you feel will have a big impact on your energy. You might have noticed that spending time with some friends leaves you feeling topped up and raring to go, while hanging out with others leaves you feeling drained and despondent. Consider who in your life is a radiator (someone who inspires feelings of positivity and joy) and who is a drain (someone whom you feel tired and depleted after spending time with).

Like many of us, I'm all too familiar with feeling obligated to maintain relationships that don't serve me, out of a sense of duty or a fear of conflict. However, it's crucial that we give ourselves permission to set boundaries and prioritise the relationships that truly nourish and support us. (We'll talk more about boundaries and how to set them in Chapter Eight.) Still, if you can't or don't want to avoid the drains in your life, think about the type of recharging activities you might need to engage in after spending time with them.

Give Yourself the Rest You Need

In sum, to give ourselves the best foundation upon which to achieve our own vision of success, we need to focus not just on physical rest but on all the types of activities explored in this chapter. And I'm a big believer that we can't just hope that these opportunities to recharge will come—we need to be proactive in planning and making arrangements for them.

Before we start that planning, let's explore how your productivity archetype might impact your relationship with resting and recharging. What we value and how we're motivated will influence the things we prioritise in all areas of life, and that is also true of rest. I see this play out regularly with my clients. In fact,

I've never worked with anyone who feels fully recharged in all four quadrants. Here are some things to keep in mind depending on your productivity archetype.

The Doer

In my experience, women who identify as doers generally fill their calendars with activities that sit in the high-stimulation quadrants, but they find it more difficult to prioritise activities that will help them feel physically recharged. Doers might avoid these activities because they seem less productive or important than the other activities, just as I did, but it's vital to acknowledge that when we don't prioritise physically recharging, we run the risk of hampering our performance and actually becoming less productive.

If you identify as a doer, assess your schedule for the coming week and consider what you need to change to ensure you can get enough sleep. Make "get enough sleep" a goal on your to-do list if that helps. Remember, taking care of yourself is not a luxury but a necessity.

The Perfectionist

I've found that women who identify as perfectionists often struggle most with activities that fall into the creative-recharge quadrant, and that's because there doesn't tend to be a blueprint for how to engage in these sorts of activities perfectly. While we can build activities like journaling, sleeping, or exercising into a routine we may aspire to complete daily, tasks like walking in nature or experiencing art can feel more nebulous. Or perhaps we might hesitate to try to learn a new skill or check out a creative class because we suspect our output might not reach the standards we have for ourselves.

If that resonates, I've got a task for you: visit somewhere in the town or city where you live and challenge yourself to see it as if you'd never laid eyes on it before. Visiting somewhere that's familiar to you should feel less overwhelming, but giving yourself the focus to see it through the eyes of a tourist might help you recharge creatively.

The Dreamer

Women who identify as dreamers tend to be drawn to activities in the high-stimulation quadrants, drawing inspiration from getting out and about or scribbling down endless ideas during a journaling session. But they're not always as proactive at making time for the activities that help them mentally and emotionally recharge, and this can negatively impact their productivity levels, especially as stress or tiredness can take their toll on their levels of confidence and self-belief.

The advice I always give dreamers when it comes to recharging is to focus on the basics. Getting enough sleep or squeezing in some exercise doesn't always seem that exciting, especially when your mind is buzzing with ideas, but they will help you build the resources that make it easier to take action. Try to let go of any guilt that comes with prioritising these basic needs. A good way to do this can be to endeavour to treat yourself like a toddler, remembering that fresh air, sleep, and good nutrition are all essential elements of positive well-being.

The Procrastinator

In my experience supporting women who identify as procrastinators, they often struggle to prioritise activities that fall into the mental-recharge quadrant the most. They start off with all the best intentions—buying a new journal, downloading a meditation app, or borrowing a recommended book from the library—but when it comes to actually sitting down to write, meditate, or read, they may find themselves distracted by other tasks, such as putting the laundry away or scrolling social media.

If this resonates and you want to start engaging with these activities—and reaping the benefits that doing so will bring—my advice is to start small and stack. Starting small is self-explanatory: instead of challenging yourself to read a whole chapter or fill three pages in your journal, focus on simply doing the thing for five minutes and building up from there. Stacking refers to adding the habit onto something you already do every day. For example, I start each day with a cup of tea, and I leave my journal in the kitchen so that I can scribble down a few thoughts while the kettle is boiling, thus stacking it onto my tea drinking. The easier you can make an activity, the more likely you will be to take action.

Giving ourselves the opportunity to feel fully rested and recharged requires us to reconnect with our needs and think about what is required to meet them. We will all have some areas that we gravitate towards more naturally than others, but it's important to take a step back and check in across the board rather than let our usual preferences lead the way. Otherwise, whether we are highly productive or barely getting our tasks done, we'll find that joy has been neglected.

DO IT YOUR WAY

Below you will find a blank example of the rest-and-recharge model. Take some time to jot down activities that you would enjoy in each quadrant.

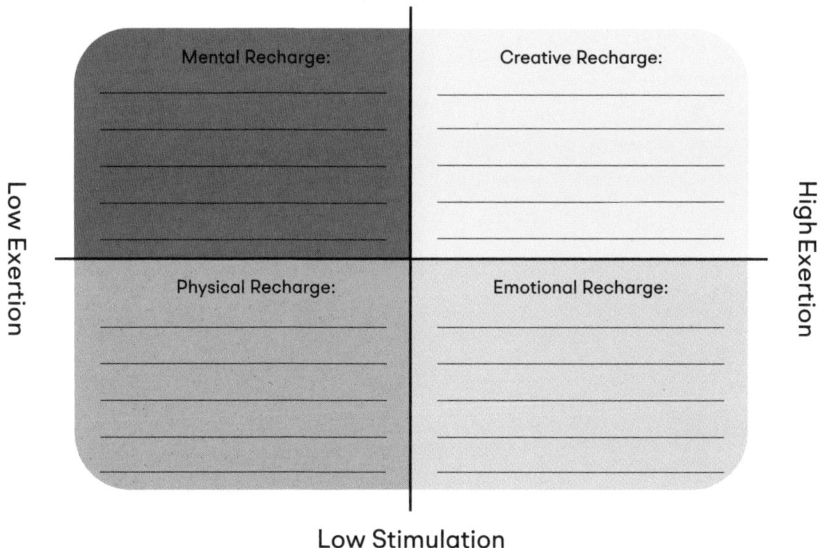

Then, check in with how mentally, physically, creatively, and emotionally recharged you currently feel. Use this information to create your own personalised rest-and-recharge plan. Pro tip: don't forget to consider how other people will factor into your plan!

Prioritise Rest in a World That Values Busyness

Before we wrap up this chapter, I want to acknowledge that it's not always easy to prioritise rest and the activities that will recharge us in a world that values busyness, especially as women.

A few months ago, I hosted a workshop for some clients on how to set and communicate boundaries. We talked about why boundaries are important and explored the boundaries that my clients felt were necessary for them to thrive. One client identified that she wanted to keep at least one weekend a month free of any plans, something that she believed would give her some much-needed time to rest and recalibrate during what has felt like an intense season of life for her. She knew the boundary she wanted to set, and she knew why setting it would be beneficial for her, but she still struggled with the thought of putting it into action. "What should I say," she asked me, "when people want to know why I can't meet up? How can I turn down their invitations if I don't actually have anything else in the calendar?"

Her quandary perfectly summed up the problem we face as women when it comes to prioritising rest: we feel like we can do it only if we've got a valid excuse. I noticed this myself when I was pregnant with my daughter—I found it so much easier to say no and communicate my need for rest because I knew that others would understand. But here's the thing: we do not need anybody else's blessing to start giving ourselves the rest we crave. We do not need to justify our need for downtime or pretend to others that we can cope without rest. Rest isn't optional—it's an essential part of our mental and physical health and a key requirement for us to be able to perform at our best.

And yet I know that even if you agree wholeheartedly with me, you may struggle with putting this value into practice. If that feels true, I want to share a piece of advice that changed the game for me. In her brilliant book *Untamed*, Glennon Doyle (2020) writes, "There is no such thing as one-way liberation." And that's what I like to remember when it comes to making choices that perhaps feel scary or new, choices that go against those that have been modelled to us by others: when we make a brave choice, we pave the way for others to do the same thing. In the case of rest, when we prioritise meeting our own rest needs, we show others that it is safe for them to do so. It doesn't make it feel any less uncomfortable to go against the grain, but it can provide an important reminder of why we're doing that.

If we want to live in a world that prioritises rest above busyness, we need to play our role in building that world. We can do that by giving ourselves permission to choose rest, even when it feels uncomfortable to do so. Rest is a radical act, especially as a woman. To choose to validate our own needs and deem ourselves worthy of joy, fulfilment, and care, no matter how much we have done to earn it, is an act of resistance. Imagine how the world might be different if 52 percent of the population stopped putting themselves at the bottom of the to-do list and instead showed themselves the same amount of care and attention they show everybody else. Imagine how the structures and societies we exist within might change for the better if we all felt recharged—mentally, physically, creatively, and emotionally.

That is the type of world that I want to live in, and I'm committed to playing my part in building it by prioritising my own need for rest—will you join me?

LET IT GO

Sometimes, finding the space and time to rest means saying no. What do you need to let go of to create more time for rest? Here are some ideas to get you thinking:

- What activities do you currently give your time to that might feel restful on the surface but don't actually replenish your energy in any way? For example, scrolling social media or listening to a true-crime podcast might actually increase your stress levels rather than diminish them.
- What are you doing simply because it fits with your idea of what a superwoman would do? For example, committing to cooking all your meals from scratch when your family would be more than happy to get takeout once a week.
- What boundaries do you need to set with others to create more time for quality rest? Remember that this can be as simple as letting friends know you'll be offline at a certain time or asking your partner to help out for thirty minutes while you head out for a jog.

LET'S RECAP

- It can be tempting to sacrifice rest in favour of getting more done, but research has shown that rest is key for productivity, especially for women who often juggle multiple roles and responsibilities.
- We need more than just physical rest to feel fully recharged. We also need to recharge mentally, creatively, and emotionally.
- We may find it easier to prioritise some quadrants of the rest-and-recharge model than others depending on our productivity archetype.
- It can be difficult to prioritise resting and recharging in a world that values busyness, but it's essential if we want to make a change.

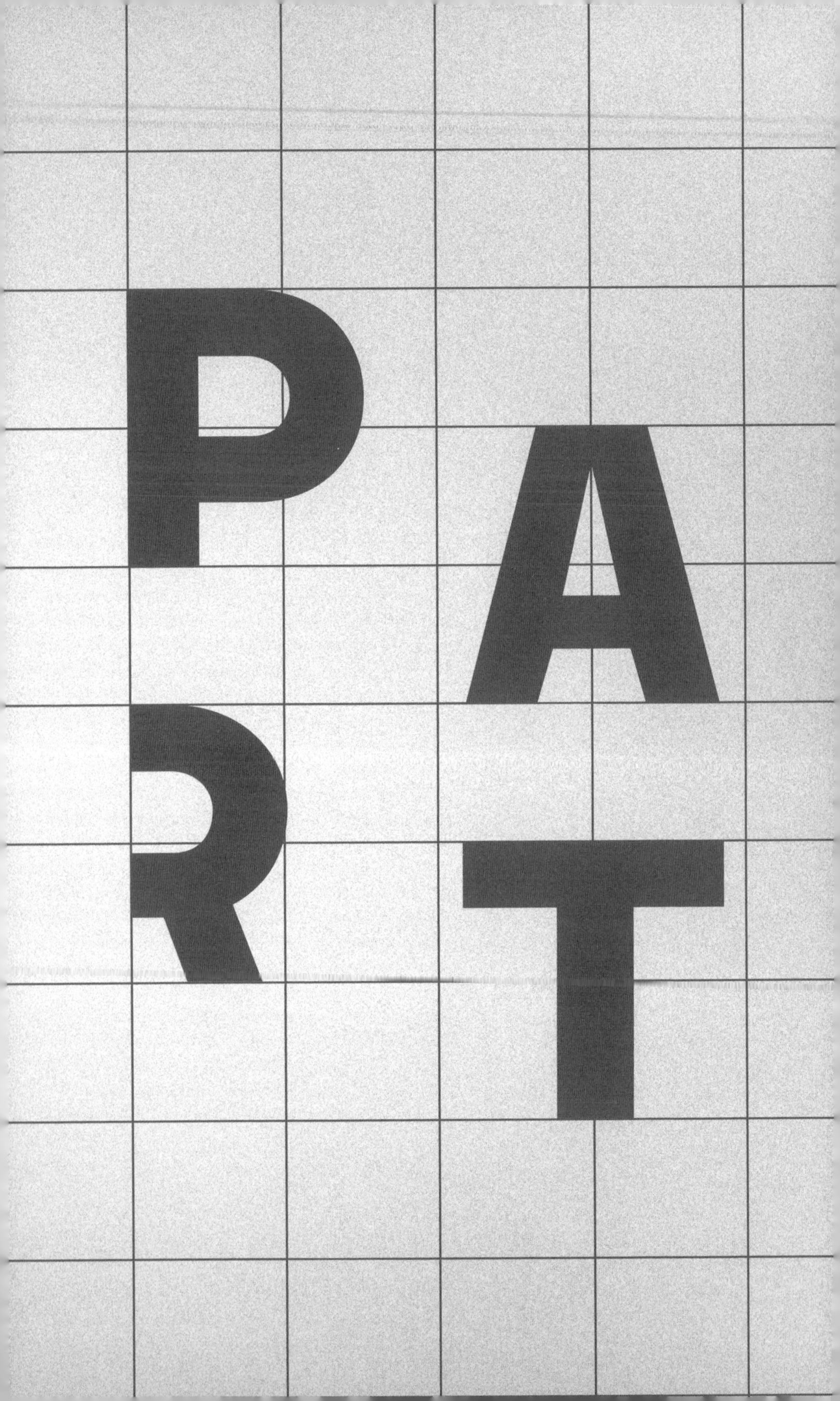
PART

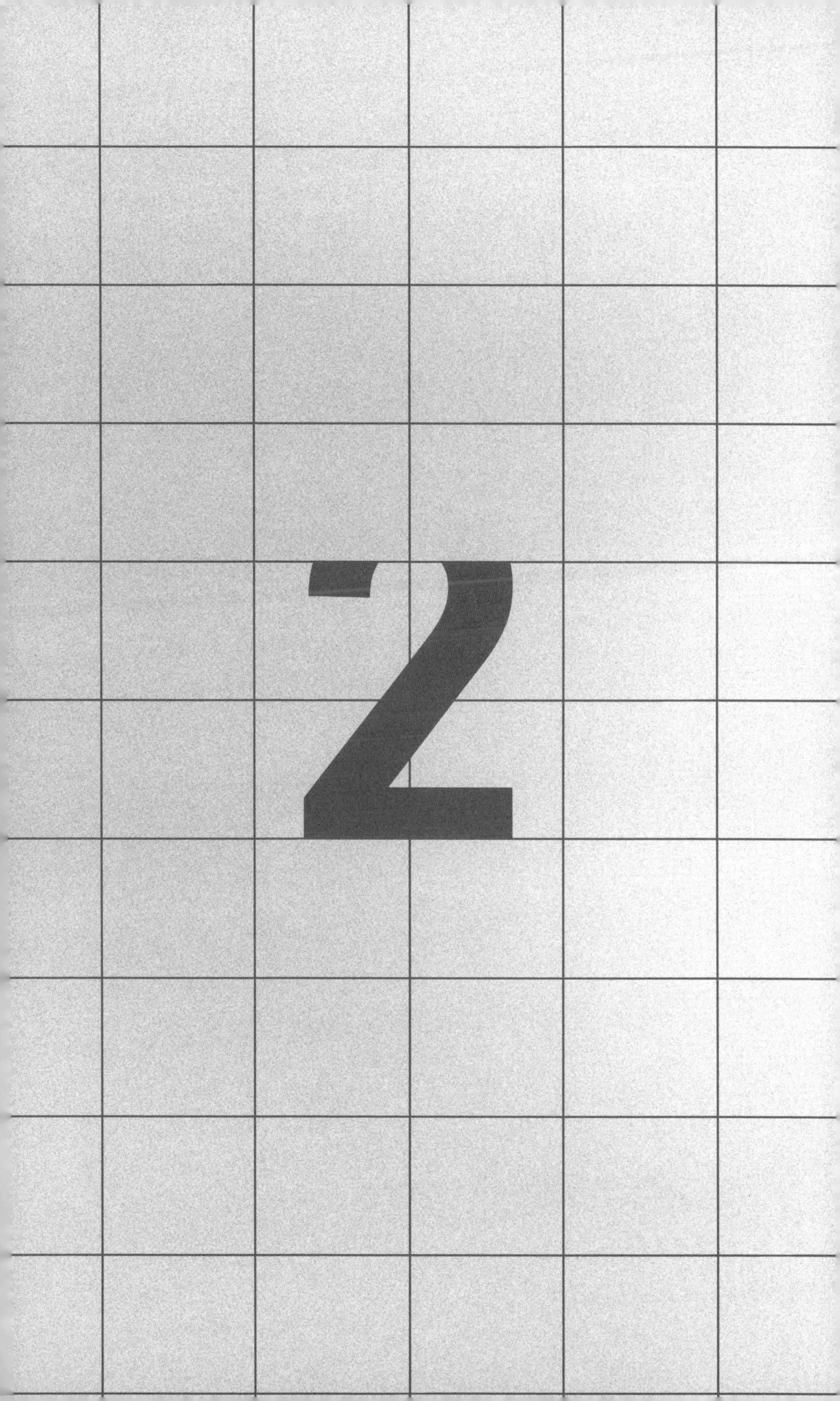
2

CHAPTER 5:

HARNESS YOUR UNIQUE ENERGY CYCLES

For as long as I can remember, I have had to work hard at my creativity. I love to make things—to develop workshops, to create useful content, to write—but it always feels like it requires a lot of effort and discipline on my part. Developing the idea for my first book, *Choose Joy*, took months of back-and-forth and many rounds of revisions with my patient editors to arrive at an outline we were happy with.

So, the way the idea for this book arrived felt surprising and unfamiliar. I was out for a walk on my lunch break, heading to a local café to grab a sandwich before an afternoon of coaching calls, when the idea hit me, fully formed. It was a bizarre feeling, and one I don't think I'd ever had before. The concept arrived so urgently and completely that I found myself furiously typing notes on my phone while I waited in line at the café, scared that it would leave just as quickly as it had appeared.

The experience was strange for many reasons. Firstly, I hadn't been consciously thinking about a second book—my first still hadn't been published, and I was working on some other projects that were more pressing. The other thing that made it unusual was that I was twenty-two weeks pregnant, and I had spent the previous four months feeling bone-tired and trying my best not to throw up. My productivity and creativity had been at an all-time low, with even replying to the simplest of emails feeling like an arduous task. But as I entered the middle of my second trimester, I realised something had changed. I was enjoying a sense of energy and flow that I hadn't experienced since I was a child.

From speaking to friends, I realised that my experience wasn't unique. One friend told me that during that stage of her pregnancy, she had been more productive than ever before, tackling tasks on her to-do list that had been untouched for years. Another told me that she'd argued with her husband almost daily during the second trimester because he kept telling her to slow down and rest, while she felt better than ever. I could understand her point. Rather than wanting to take things easy, I felt charged up and ready to go, go, go.

Of course, not everybody feels this way: My sister, who was pregnant at the same time as I was, struggled with ongoing sickness and found my boundless energy downright annoying. My doctor explained to me that a combination of the placenta starting to work, lessening the energetic toll placed on the pregnant person, and a rebalancing of hormones often leads to a spell of vitality and vibrancy during this period. I certainly experienced that. The proposal for this book wasn't the only thing I managed to get done during those energetic weeks. I also powered through business admin tasks, redecorated two rooms in our home, recorded the audiobook for my first book, and kept on top of my usual workload too.

The reason I share this anecdote isn't to brag or gain praise for how productive I was during my pregnancy. In fact, I believe that celebrating the productivity of pregnant women rather than giving them space to manage such a huge physical and emotional transition is just another way that hustle culture does us dirty. I decided to write about my second-trimester experience because it changed the way that I thought about energy.

Energy management is something I have been interested in and researching for a long time. Until I had that burst of productivity during my pregnancy, I'd always thought of energy management as a sort of mathematical equation, a formula of sorts where you can tweak some variables and change the outcome. I'd approached it in the same way as I'd approached time management—trying to control every bit of the process in the quest to free up as much energy as possible. Prioritising sleep in the hope that I'd wake up more well rested. Expending a bit of energy on exercise, trusting that I'd experience a return on my investment. Trying to eat a more balanced diet to see if it could help me avoid a midafternoon slump.

And of course, things like nutrition, sleep, and movement all play a role in managing our energy, just like planning and calendar blocking can help us manage our time better. But what my experience during pregnancy taught me is that seeing energy management as a simple equation misses the full picture. I was curious: Are there other factors at play that impact our energy, things that we aren't paying enough attention to—hormones, for example, or seasons, or working patterns, or our natural energetic rhythms? Just like we've already explored, we're not robots or machines who can be precisely controlled or managed; we're humans who exist in different bodies, environments, and contexts.

It got me thinking—what if the key to getting more done in a way that feels good to me isn't by relying on discipline or some newfangled productivity hack but rather by accepting that my body and environment are important factors to be considered? What if the route to more joyful productivity lies in identifying my own energy cycles and making them work for me rather than against me?

The Impact of Hormones

Given that my thinking on this topic of energy management evolved from a set of hormones working together to deliver me a significant energy surge, exploring the impact of hormones on our productivity levels is the perfect place to start. For as long as I can remember, I'd only ever thought about hormones in a negative context. They'd get the blame whenever I was feeling angry or melancholy before my menstrual cycle was about to begin, and once I was even asked if I was "feeling hormonal" by a male boss when I assertively shared a frustration in a meeting—an experience that still makes my blood boil to this day. I grew up believing that my hormones were a weakness or a hindrance to overcome, a belief very much instilled in me by popular culture and society, so I had never once considered how they might impact my energy or productivity, or how I might harness them to help me. But learning more about hormone cycles was transformative for me.

Before I dive into how our hormones can impact our energy, let's first recap the difference between typical male and female hormonal cycles. Of course, this is just a snapshot, and it would be impossible to factor in all the nuances, complexities, and quirks that can come with this topic—let alone do justice to the vast variety of lived experiences—in the space we've got available, but I still think it's worth exploring here. I also want to acknowledge that the terms male and female in this context refer to the sex assigned at birth, but of course, sex and gender exist on a spectrum. While we will explore how specific hormones impact our energy, individual experiences may vary. If for these, or any other, reasons this section doesn't feel useful to you, please feel free to skip it.

Let's start with the typical male hormonal cycle. The main hormone that impacts a male body is testosterone, and a full cycle is completed every twenty-four hours, with testosterone levels being highest in the morning and decreasing steadily throughout the day before replenishing again overnight. This means that people with a male hormonal cycle will typically feel most energetic in the morning and will gradually get more tired throughout the day as those testosterone levels start to decrease. And as the cycle repeats every twenty-four hours, they're likely to have a similar amount of energy each day (Lichterman n.d.).

People who experience a menstrual cycle, on the other hand, experience a more complicated hormonal cycle. Rather than repeating every twenty-four hours, it takes around twenty-eight days for a menstrual hormone cycle to complete. Those twenty-eight days can be split into four phases: menstruation, the follicular phase, ovulation, and the luteal phase. As with the male cycle, the female cycle has a whole cocktail of hormones at work, with the major players driving this cycle being oestrogen, progesterone, and testosterone.

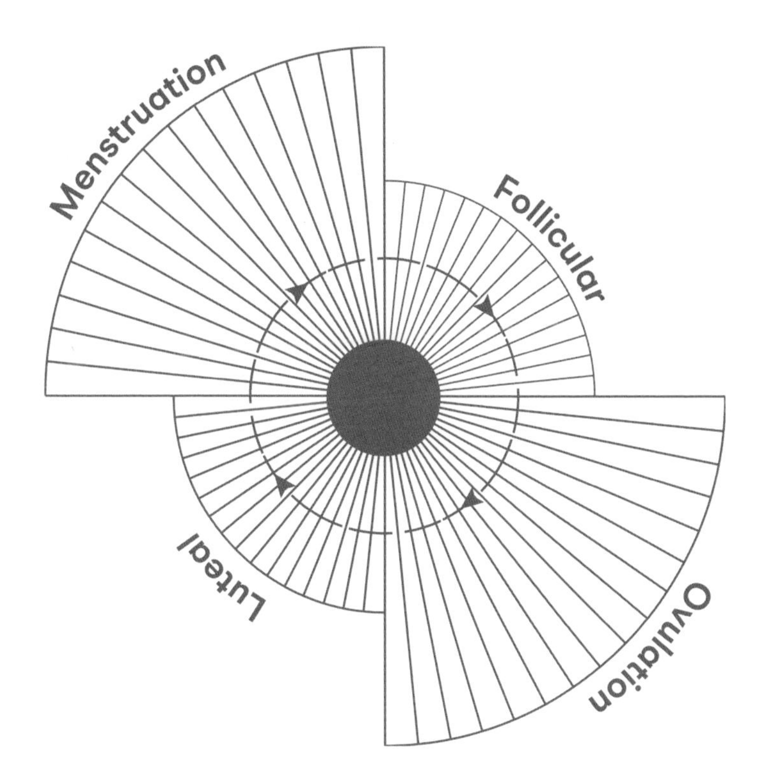

In the first phase of the cycle, menstruation, hormones are at their lowest point, meaning that energy levels are likely to be low. If you have a menstrual cycle, this is the time of the month when you might feel less sociable and more anxious. However, it's not all bad—this phase of the cycle can be a great time for reflecting and assessing your priorities.

In the second phase, the follicular phase, oestrogen—affectionately named *the Beyoncé hormone* in *Period Power* by Maisie Hill (2019)—starts to rise, and with it, your energy, enthusiasm for life, and self-confidence. This is likely to be a positive and optimistic time in the cycle, when you find it easy to plan, explore new hobbies, or start building a new habit.

The third phase, ovulation, is when oestrogen and testosterone are at their peaks. This is likely to be your most energetic time, and your productivity, ability to find joy, and communication skills will all be at their best. This is a great time for presentations, parties, and big projects, as your hormones will be working together to make you feel pretty invincible.

Following ovulation, oestrogen drops sharply, and the luteal phase begins. This decrease in oestrogen can lead to a slump in energy, interrupting those productive vibes you might have been enjoying during ovulation. In the luteal phase, progesterone increases, leaving you feeling quieter, more sensitive, foggy, and more inwardly focused. This can be a challenging phase, but it can also be a time when you feel more connected with yourself, making it a great time to get in touch with your intuition (Lichterman n.d.).

Another way of thinking about the menstrual cycle is to compare it to nature's seasons. Menstruation can be thought of as the winter of our cycle, a time when we have little energy and want to be cosy at home. The follicular phase is like spring, when we start to see our energy and optimism return. Ovulation mirrors summer, when everything feels good and we are at our most vibrant. Finally, you can think of the luteal phase as fall, a time when you might start to retreat and become more introspective.

When I first learnt about the differences in the male and female hormone cycles, my first thought was this: it really is a man's world. Everything about the way we operate in Western societies is designed with the male hormonal cycle in mind, and I have no doubt that it's one of the core reasons why we put pressure on ourselves to perform at the same level every day. If the people designing the system are experiencing a hormonal cycle that repeats every twenty-four hours—waking up each day with a similar amount of energy—then it makes sense that we would expect ourselves to produce, work, and create with consistency. But what happens if your energy cycle doesn't match the one that we've built our systems and norms around?

Well, in my experience, it becomes a trigger for our old friend the shame-and-blame cycle. For years, I have beaten myself up for experiencing an energy slump, telling myself that the problem must be that I'm lazy, unmotivated, or undisciplined. When my self-confidence has dipped, rather than understanding that this is often caused by a dip in oestrogen, I have internalised it as a sign that I'm not good enough. I've worried that I don't have the commitment or dedication to achieve my goals, and I've blamed myself for not always being able to operate at the same rate as my male peers. I've wallowed in the guilt and shame that come with that, when all along, I was simply experiencing the natural side effects of my biology.

Have you ever found yourself doing the same thing? Learning about the impact our hormones have on our energy levels was transformative for me for a number of reasons. Firstly, I started to get to know myself so much better. Tracking how I felt at different parts of my cycle helped me spot patterns and gain a greater understanding of why I experienced energetic and emotional ebbs and flows throughout the month. For example, I know that on days five through eleven of my cycle, when oestrogen starts to build, I feel like a superwoman, ticking off items on my to-do list with ease, while in the last week or so, when my progesterone levels rise, I feel particularly sensitive to criticism. Having this understanding has helped me unlock a level of self-compassion that I'd been unable to find before. Now, when I'm struggling to get going in the morning or I'm finding that simple tasks require more effort, I can recognise that it's not some sort of moral failing on my part but instead my body performing a function that has been part of our biology for thousands of years. It also helps me take measures that protect me—for example, reducing my social media intake when I'm feeling more sensitive and vulnerable to comparison. In addition, I can now see that my hormone cycle comes with its own in-built superpowers. Sure, I don't have the same energy every single day like some of my male counterparts, but what I do have is a rhythm that I can harness, embracing the world-domination vibes that come during the follicular phase to help me get shit done. I also feel empowered to lean into the more intuitive and reflective parts of my cycle to help me think deeply and create.

A client of mine had a similar experience. Hattie strongly identified as a doer—she had scaled the career ranks quickly and, at the age of thirty, was heading up a large team at a global consulting firm. To the outside world, Hattie looked like the epitome of success, but that's not how she felt. Despite her achievements, she was riddled with self-doubt and experienced regular periods of low mood. The way Hattie dealt with this was to work harder and harder, and she struggled to give herself permission to rest—even her weekends were scheduled months in advance. Learning more about how her menstrual cycle and hormones might be impacting her was an emotional experience for Hattie. She was able to better understand why some weeks she felt like she could run the world and why in others she struggled with even the most basic of tasks. She cried in our coaching session, grieving for all the times she'd beaten herself up for not being able to sustain her productivity levels. In her words, "Why aren't we taught this stuff at school?!" But the insight gave her optimism too—having this knowledge was the permission slip she needed to schedule more physical rest when she needed it most. Now, she is able to trust that this need for rest isn't laziness and that it isn't going to hold her back. Hattie also found that knowing more about how her hormonal cycle impacted her energy levels created an opportunity to map her workload in-line with it, and she scheduled reflective work for the menstrual phase and anything higher octane for her follicular or ovulation phase. And during those times when she couldn't influence her workload and when her schedule required she complete tasks that didn't sync as well with the stage of her cycle as she'd have liked, she was able to be more compassionate and kinder to herself. But perhaps the biggest takeaway for Hattie was that, in understanding why she was feeling the way she was, she was able to stop seeing herself as a problem to be solved, reducing the amount of energy she expended each month trying to force herself into new routines to tackle her low mood or sluggishness.

And I think that's the important takeaway here. Our hormones impact our energy in a big way, and for some women that impact is greater than others. For example, according to the Edge Foundation (n.d.), women with ADHD are more sensitive to declines in oestrogen and may be at a higher risk of experiencing anxiety, depression, forgetfulness, and other symptoms during certain phases of their cycle (or during menopause) as a result. Other conditions such as PMDD (premenstrual dysphoric disorder) or endometriosis, which impacts 10 percent of women worldwide, can exacerbate the negative impacts of experiencing a menstrual cycle (Endometriosis UK, n.d.). I have one friend who is so riddled with pain due to her endometriosis that she struggles to get out of bed when her symptoms are at their worst. I've also watched friends be floored by fertility treatments and the swathes of hormone injections involved.

The impact our hormones can have on our energy is immense, and yet we still have a long way to go in acknowledging this as a society, especially given that periods, menopause, and fertility are still often treated as taboo topics. For this reason, it might not always be possible to make huge changes to accommodate the ways in which our energy ebbs and flows. And while I'm a strong believer that we need workplace policies that better support women with these challenges, we're not there just yet. And of course, it will be even more challenging to honour your natural energetic rhythms if you face systemic barriers, discrimination, or a lack of resources and support, as many women do. But when we recognise and acknowledge that it's not just our willpower or determination impacting our ability to tackle the to-do list, we can stop the self-blame and, in doing so, free up a lot more energy and focus to pour into the things that are important to us. And when we face the fact that we're not all built the same way, we can begin to advocate for greater equity and inclusion in the workplace and society as a whole.

If we're redefining our success on our own terms, perhaps it's time to stop subscribing to society's often unrealistic expectations and, instead, give our well-being greater value than we do our output.

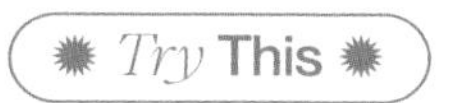

Have a go at tracking your energy for a month. If you have a menstrual cycle, start on the first day of your period. If you don't have one, you could track your energy in-line with the lunar calendar or simply start on the first of the month. Then every day for a month, write down one line to describe how you're feeling and what your mood and energy levels are like on each day. You might choose to repeat this for a couple of months so that you can get a clear picture of any patterns.

Then, use the following prompts to reflect:

- What have you noticed about how your energy changes throughout the month?
- Is there a time of the month when you feel most energised? What feels easy to you in this phase?
- Is there a time of the month when you feel most tired? What feels hard to you in this phase?
- Are there any tweaks you could make to your schedule to honour the patterns you've spotted? For example, scheduling social events with friends during the more energetic parts of your cycle or making your workout routine gentler during the times of the month when you may be feeling more tired.
- What might happen to your productivity levels if you were to lean into your energy fluctuations instead of trying to resist them? What might be possible for you?
- How might practising greater self-compassion as your energy ebbs and flows change your experience?

Night Owl or Early Bird?

Another thing I noticed when I started to get curious about energy management was the discourse about early risers versus night owls. For as long as I can remember, every interview I've read with a "successful" person includes a reflection about how getting up early is their key to getting everything done, and for a long time, I believed that this would be my path to productivity too. I had internalised the belief that to get everything on my to-do list done I needed to be up and on with it at five a.m., and I tried for years to do just that. I read a book called *The 5am Club*, set my alarm earlier, and even bought one of those fancy lamps that is supposed to help you wake up naturally by making the light in your room mimic a sunrise. And yet I could still never manage being an early bird for more than a couple of days at a time. On those days, I'd be so exhausted and wired from the caffeine required to get through the day that I struggled to do anything of value after around two p.m.

I've also noticed that while the early risers are celebrated in the media, many of the successful people in my own life don't align with the morning-person pattern. For example, one of my brilliant clients finds that she's so energetic during the hours of ten a.m. to one p.m. that she can get away with working for only three hours a day if she schedules her tasks during that time. And my friend who works as a marketing director finds that her creativity doesn't really get going until around eight p.m., when everyone else in her house is winding down. So, I was curious, is becoming an early bird really the secret to being more productive, or is it all a bit more complex than that?

My research led me to discover something called sleep chronotypes. Sleep chronotypes are a way of categorising your natural disposition to feel sleepy or more energised at different times of the day. And rather than being a preference or something that is influenced by your routine, your sleep chronotype is genetic—when you feel most energised comes down to the length of your PER3 gene (Archer et al. 2003). It's theorised that we evolved to have different chronotypes in the population because it was essential for survival during our hunter-gatherer era—sleeping at different times meant there would always be someone on the lookout for danger (Samson et al. 2017).

I'd heard of early birds and night owls before, but it turns out that there are four sleep chronotypes—the bear, the lion, the wolf, and the dolphin.

- **THE BEAR** is the most common chronotype, and people who fall into this category get up when the sun rises and fall asleep when the sun sets. They tend to be productive all day but may experience a midafternoon slump.
- **THE LION** is what we would usually call an early bird. They wake up energised and ready to start the day and do their best work in the mornings.
- **THE WOLF** is similar to a night owl and has a strong preference for evenings, as this is when they really get going. They tend to struggle with mornings and may find it challenging to fit into society's typical schedules.
- **THE DOLPHIN** is the rarest chronotype, making up around 10 percent of people (Calm 2024). Dolphins tend to struggle with insomnia, finding themselves tired during the day and wired at night. Their productivity sweet spot tends to be late afternoon and early evenings.

Interestingly, our chronotype tends to change throughout our lives. Children often have early chronotypes (for example, the lion), but this shifts towards a later chronotype during our adolescence (yes, your teenager has a legitimate biological reason to sleep in late), before shifting back again in adulthood.

Just like learning about the impact of our hormones on our energy cycles, learning about sleep chronotypes felt like a major lightbulb moment for me. And again, gaining this knowledge felt equal parts empowering and frustrating. It was great to be able to identify my chronotype and understand more about what that meant for my energy levels and natural productivity sweet spots, but if our energetic rhythms are controlled by our genetics and are something that we can't control with discipline or willpower, why are we repeatedly told that the best way to get more done is to get up earlier? Why are our working patterns so inflexible? I found myself asking the same question as my client Hattie: Why aren't we taught this stuff in school?

The COVID-19 pandemic presented many challenges for women—data shows that one of the key economic impacts of the pandemic was widening the gender disparity in the labour market (Barua 2022)—but for some, it presented the opportunity to work in alignment with our sleep chronotypes for the first time. This was the case for my client Naomi. As a single parent to two young children, Naomi faced greater challenges than most during the lockdowns, with the responsibility for childcare and homeschooling falling squarely on her shoulders. Despite the stress and challenges COVID-19 presented, Naomi found it to be a fruitful time for her career, with increased flexibility meaning that she could change up her work pattern and get more done in the evenings when she was naturally more energised and focused. Unfortunately for Naomi, the organisation she works for recently rescinded their flexible working policy, ordering staff back to the office and implementing the old nine-to-five working pattern. Naomi feels that this has hampered not just the enjoyment of her work but her productivity too—she told me that even though she has more support with her children and domestic duties now, she's never experienced quite the same flow with her work as she had during the lockdowns.

Just like with hormones, it seems we're not quite ready yet as a society to accept that we all have variations in our daily energetic rhythms. But even if you don't have the flexibility to shift your working patterns, or if you have other responsibilities, such as caregiving, that require you to structure your day in a way that doesn't work best for you, simply knowing which sleep chronotype you identify as can change your inner dialogue and your expectations of yourself for the better.

DO IT YOUR WAY

Using the information shared above, identify which sleep chronotype you feel most aligned with in this stage of your life.

Consider how your sleep chronotype might impact your energy levels and opportunities for productivity, and how you might tweak your schedule to make accommodations for it. For example, if you identify as a wolf, is there a way to make sure your most creative and high-energy tasks are saved for the end of the day?

The Impact of Seasons

We talked about how our hormonal cycle can mirror the seasonal cycle, but what impact do the actual seasons have on our energy levels? If you live in a place that experiences seasons, the variation in daylight hours, temperature, and abundance in nature can be vast, and this can lead to fluctuations in your productivity. Before the advent of electricity, this was recognised in the way we worked—months that were filled with daylight were busy, with tasks like planting, farming, and harvesting all completed then, and the darker, colder months took a slower pace, with more time spent at home preserving and resting. Nowadays, however, there is little seasonality to our working patterns, with most of us working the same number of hours in winter as we do in summer, give or take the odd national holiday or week of vacation.

This expectation to produce as though we are in continual summer is just another way that our societal structures expect us to act more like robots than humans. As the saying goes, nothing in nature blooms all year round, and yet we expect ourselves to, and inevitably that takes a toll. While not everybody will experience fluctuations in mood or energy throughout the year, there are certainly trends that suggest plenty of people do. For example, Google Trend UK data shows that searches for the phrase *recovering from burnout* are at their highest during the second week of January, the deepest point of winter, when daylight hours are at their lowest. Similarly, searches for the phrase *am I depressed?* are at their lowest in July and August, a time when the days are longer and warmer, and many people take a break from work.

Additionally, the pressures and loads women carry may also increase during certain points of the year. For example, research shows that women in heterosexual relationships take on the majority of labour during the holiday period (Reese 2019)—from ensuring the home is kept clean and tidy to shopping for gifts and *kinkeeping* (the act of maintaining and strengthening familial ties). And if you have caregiving responsibilities, you might find that the mental and physical loads fluctuate with the seasons. As the parent of an energetic toddler, I've certainly found that winter feels like more of a slog, with fewer daylight hours meaning that we spend more time at home. This struggle might be even greater if you care for someone with disabilities or health challenges that are exacerbated in different seasons.

You might not relate to the trends or patterns I've shared here (in the past, I have found winter to be a more productive time, likely because I respond well to routine, which feels more absent in my life in the summer months), but the chances are that you will experience some fluctuation throughout the year. Think back to the last few years. Is there a certain month or season when you feel more energised, and is there a time when you're more likely to feel exhausted? How is your creativity or motivation impacted by the shifting seasons? Again, when we acknowledge that our energy might be impacted by what is happening outside our window, we can accommodate seasonal energy changes and manage them better. For example, if you struggle with winter, you might find it more impactful to avoid setting resolutions in January and instead save any new goals for the springtime, when you have the energy to take the action needed. Or if the warm summer temperatures leave you feeling drained, perhaps you might prefer to schedule trips or social events in the cooler months.

Other Factors That Might Impact Your Energy

I hope by now you can see that managing our energy is complicated, and that hormones, chronotypes, and nature all play a role in how productive we may feel at any given point. But of course, even that is not a complete list, and there are all sorts of factors that might impact how energetic or productive you feel on any given day. Here are a few other ideas that might be worth considering:

- Your working patterns: How does the structure of your workweek impact your energy? For example, if you are a hybrid worker, do you feel more energised from being around your colleagues in the office, or does the commute exhaust you? You can use this information to help you balance your workload for the week.
- Your health: If you suffer from a chronic health condition, it's likely that you'll experience fluctuations in your energy depending on your overall health. Accepting and accommodating your need for rest and using more energetic periods as opportunities to get ahead will likely feel more empowering than expecting yourself to perform at the same level every day. It may also be empowering to acknowledge that you don't have the same energy levels as those around you and accommodate this in your own personal definition of success.
- Your routines as a caregiver: If you're a parent or guardian or if you give care in any other capacity, the chances are that the routines of your dependents may play a role in influencing your energy. For example, I know that if my daughter is unwell or going through a tricky patch with sleep, my overall energy will be compromised. Similarly, having to travel a lot to care for an elderly or unwell relative may also take its toll.
- Holidays and traditions: Annual holidays and traditions can also play a big role in your overall energy levels. You might find that you experience an energy surge after taking a break in the summer but feel stretched more thinly during the festive period. Again, acknowledging this and planning your activities in-line with those fluctuations will make life feel much easier.

Take some time to consider what else might impact your energy and how you can stay mindful of that as you move throughout the month or year. You might also like to reflect on your definition of success and explore how you can incorporate your energetic fluctuations into your vision for a joyful life.

Productivity Archetypes and Energy

One last thing I want to explore before we start to wrap up this chapter is how knowing more about our productivity archetype might help us better manage our energy. Below, you can see each archetype's energetic superpowers and watch-outs. I have also included a task or new perspective to help you manage your energy better based on your archetype. As we've discussed, there are all sorts of factors that come into play, so you might not identify with everything written about your productivity archetype, but take the time to notice what does ring true to you.

The Doer

Doers are the most naturally energetic of all the productivity archetypes. They find it easy to get started with something new, and because they're motivated by completing tasks, they can usually sustain energy well throughout a project. However, they're at risk of being so busy that they don't notice shifts in their energetic rhythms as a result of factors such as hormone cycles or seasons. This can lead them to push through on little energy, resulting in disappointment in themselves and even burnout. Remember my client Hattie, whom I mentioned earlier? This is what happened to her, and it's something I've also experienced myself. Nowadays, I try to give myself more space and time to check in with how I'm feeling. I'm also more considerate of my energetic peaks when planning projects—even if I don't have the control to plan all my tasks according to my energy, I can be more mindful of when I'll need additional rest, or when to be more aware of my inner dialogue.

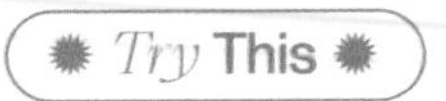

Commit to paying more attention to your energy levels. A simple way to do this is to ask yourself each morning how energetic you feel on a scale of one to ten. Checking in with your energy levels will help you notice the ebbs and flows and should make it easier to know when to push and when to be gentler with yourself.

The Perfectionist

In my experience, while perfectionists have a natural tendency to want routines and organisation, which may help them better sustain and manage their energy, they are also the archetype most likely to ignore their natural rhythms in a quest to maintain a consistent level of productivity. At times, this can make them vulnerable to negative self-talk when sticking to their plan feels difficult.

This was certainly the case for my client Rose. Rose works in finance, an industry where both women and people with the same ethnicity as she are in the minority. As a result, she felt a pressure to keep up with her peers, working late even when she was experiencing crippling stomach cramps. Rose assumed that this would make her more productive and allow her to remain competitive, but in reality, she just ended up more tired and more likely to make mistakes. This fuelled a toxic cycle where Rose would feel like she needed to work even harder to rebuild her confidence, causing her to feel even more exhausted in the long run. Since learning more about her hormonal cycle and her own natural productivity rhythms, Rose has been able to take a more flexible approach, trusting that honouring her needs will help her perform better over time. Rose told me that something that helped her make a change was acknowledging that by accepting and communicating her own limitations, not only is she better supporting her own well-being, but she is also helping create an environment where other women and people of colour in her organisation will feel safe to do the same.

Experiment with adjusting your routine in-line with one of the cycles explored in this chapter. Notice if it helps you feel better and get more of the important stuff done in the long run. Resist the urge to try to do this perfectly—you might find that you fall back into old patterns every now and then, but that's okay. It can take a while for us to settle into new changes.

The Dreamer

Dreamers often subvert energetic norms—for example, they may identify as a wolf, coming alive in the evening. This allows them to be productive at a time when others are usually resting. Additionally, dreamers are sensitive to their energetic and creative surges and are more likely to harness them than other archetypes. However, dreamers can be at risk of taking an all-or-nothing approach, getting lots done during their energetic high points but struggling to take action or make progress when they're tired or uninspired.

This was something I supported my client Phoebe with. She was tired of relying on her energetic surges to get her novel written (particularly given that as a sandwich-generation caregiver, Phoebe found the competing demands of caring for both her children and her parents meant that she experienced those surges infrequently) and recognised that in order to achieve the dreams she had mapped out for herself, she would need to find a way to be a little more consistent. Acknowledging that her energy did ebb and flow and recognising these patterns were the first steps we took, and this allowed Phoebe to trust that while she might not feel like creating every minute of every day, her energy would return. The other thing that helped Phoebe was harnessing her energetic low points more effectively, using them as a time to either find inspiration or focus on more reflective activities such as editing, or simply giving herself the time she needed to rest.

Consider how you could more effectively harness your energetic low points. Write a list of low-energy activities that inspire you or recharge your energy—for example, reading, sleeping, or journaling—and make an effort to keep prioritising these even during a fallow season. You will likely find that doing so will allow you to be even more productive when your energy returns.

The Procrastinator

Procrastinators are much better than the other productivity archetypes at protecting their energy and honouring their natural rhythms. I've noticed when supporting procrastinators that they often plan their schedule and capacity based on their energetic low points, and while this is great for protecting against burnout or exhaustion, it can mean that they aren't reaching their full potential during their more energised periods.

This is something that was becoming a major block for my client Anna as she worked on her goal of starting her own graphic design business. She knew she had the skills, and she had created a brilliant business plan, but she was struggling to find the time to take action. We realised that a big stumbling block for Anna was that she was most creative and energised in the evenings, but this tended to be when she was most busy with domestic duties, such as cooking dinner and putting her children to bed. Once Anna realised this was a block to her progress, she was able to speak to her partner about how they managed their evening routines and to free up some more time for her business.

Think of a task on your to-do list or a new habit that you've been struggling to get going with. Identify an energetic high point for you—this could be a particularly energetic time in your hormonal cycle, or a time of day when you're most energised—and see if you find it easier to make progress at that time.

LET IT GO

Given everything we've discussed in this chapter, are there any beliefs you need to let go of to help you utilise your energy better? For example, could letting go of the idea that you need to start the day strong help you embrace the fact that you're more of a night owl? Or could letting go of the need to be at your best in winter give you permission to practise the self-care you might crave at that time?

If you take just one thing away from this chapter, I want it to be this: we are all different. We exist in different bodies, with different genetics and hormones. We exist in different environments and structures, and we have different preferences that all play a role in determining our energy levels and cycles. We also each have different expectations placed on us by our cultures and communities and different systemic and structural challenges to overcome. When we acknowledge that, not only do we start to unlock clues about when we work best and when we might be at our most creative, but we can also begin to practise greater self-compassion.

I know that it isn't always straightforward to honour your own energetic rhythms. I know that there will be other factors in your life that influence how you plan your time and energy, whether those are the demands of your work schedule or the fact that you have someone in your life who relies on you to keep showing up every day, even when you're exhausted. I know that you might be sceptical about how much of a difference paying attention to all this stuff can make. But I want you to give it a go anyway. Because even if you can't flex your schedule, you can acknowledge your own humanness, and that in turn will save you all the energy you might otherwise spend beating yourself up or trying to fit a mould that isn't you.

If you've ever tried to follow somebody else's productivity tips, hacks, or schedules and struggled to make them work for you, that isn't a failure on your part. It isn't because you lack discipline or willpower or motivation or commitment—it's simply because that tip or routine wasn't grounded in your reality. So much of our world and environment has been designed with one type of energy cycle in mind, but that doesn't make your own unique energy patterns wrong. And when we accept that and begin to acknowledge and understand what our own energy cycles look like, we open ourselves up to so much possibility. Leaning into your own rhythms is a productivity hack that will actually work—and it'll feel great too. Trust me.

It's a radical act to reject the structures that society has laid out for us, but it's essential if we're going to achieve our own definition of success and start prioritising our well-being and joy in a way that we deserve. The old way of doing things wasn't designed with us in mind; let's play a part in building a new way, one that not only acknowledges our unique energetic rhythms but harnesses them to supercharge our magic.

LET'S RECAP

- Our energy levels are impacted by a wide variety of factors, including hormones, sleep chronotypes, the seasons, and our productivity archetypes.
- Male and female hormone cycles differ significantly, with a male cycle completing every twenty-four hours and a female cycle an average of twenty-eight days.
- There are four types of sleep chronotypes, determined by genetics. Your sleep chronotype impacts the time of day when you feel most productive.
- The seasons can play a big role in how productive we feel, and until fairly recently, our working patterns and expectations used to reflect this.
- We can utilise our productivity archetypes to help us manage our energy more effectively.
- It's important to acknowledge and accommodate our own energetic rhythms if we want to get more done in a way that feels joyful.

CHAPTER 6:

TRUST YOUR INTUITION TO GUIDE YOUR DECISIONS

One thing I wasn't prepared for when I had my daughter was how curious other people would be about how we were choosing to raise her. Having spent years being asked variations of the question "Do you think you'll have kids?" at every family gathering, I thought that having one might mean that I'd finally get a bit of peace and quiet. I couldn't have been more wrong—the questions increased tenfold. "Are you breastfeeding or formula feeding?" "Is she a good sleeper?" "Who do you think she looks most like?" "When are you planning to go back to work?" "Is her dad hands-on?" (Side note: notice how they never ask the dads this about mothers.) And of course: "Do you think you'll have another one?" (I was asked this just weeks after having my daughter, before my C-section scar had even begun to heal.)

But by far the question I've been asked the most since giving birth in early 2023 is this: "Is she in a good routine?" People are obsessed with baby routines, something I'd had no idea about until I got pregnant and started reading the books that friends passed on to me. It was only once my daughter arrived that I realised just what a hot topic it is. It seems that everyone has got an opinion on the routine you should adopt for your baby. Older generations will tell you about what worked best for them, fellow parents will want to compare and contrast the routine of their baby with yours, and you can't move for all the books, podcasts, or Instagram accounts trying to sell you the "perfect" routine that will finally get your child sleeping through the night.

I resisted the idea of trying to get our baby into a routine for a long time—not because I think there's anything wrong with them. In fact, I have many friends who swear that establishing one has helped their family to thrive. A routine simply didn't feel like the right fit for us. My husband and I both have fluctuating work schedules that require us to be flexible, and we liked the idea of being able to take our baby out and about with us rather than being tied to a fixed schedule. Plus, it never seemed like our little one was that keen on having one either. Her wake-up times and nap lengths were unpredictable to say the least. An added benefit was that a go-with-the-flow approach seemed to help my confidence as a new mum. Removing any fixed expectations about how the day would go meant that I wasn't beating myself up on days when things felt a little bit chaotic.

Around six months in, however, something started to change. We were stuck in a rough patch of bad sleep, and my workload was starting to creep up too. I felt overwhelmed, run-down, and more tired than I'd ever been. Whenever I mentioned this to anyone, their response was the same: "Oh, you need to get her into a routine." And so, feeling vulnerable and desperate for a bit more sleep, we tried. I found a schedule online recommended for six-month-olds, and we attempted to fit in her feeds, naps, and bedtimes accordingly. What unfolded was probably my most difficult week of parenting to date. There were tears from me, tears from my baby, and a whole bucketload of self-doubt. I woke up every morning with a pit of dread in my stomach, and I felt like a failure. Why couldn't I figure this out? Why were we struggling so much when it felt like everyone else had managed it without any stress? Had we let our baby down by not trying to establish a routine sooner?

Five or six days in, we abandoned the attempt to follow the routine I'd found online. Ironically, given that I was quitting something, the feeling of failure disappeared almost instantly. I was able to tune back into my instincts and intuition, and I felt calmer and more present with my daughter. Sure, I was still tired, but now I could see that my exhaustion wasn't because I hadn't perfected a routine but simply because I had a six-month-old, and being the parent of a small human who relies on you for all their demands is very tiring. And when we accepted that a routine wasn't going to be the magic bullet everyone told us it would be, we were able to focus on the practical changes that worked better for us—splitting the early wake-ups between my husband and me, for example, or making peace with the fact that we'd never make it to the bottom of the laundry basket. We fell back into an approach that suited us and our daughter, and I vowed to never, ever ask a fellow parent if they had a routine.

There's a reason I'm sharing this anecdote, and it isn't to present a case for or against baby routines. In fact, I couldn't really give a damn how anyone else chooses to parent or raise their kids. (It's one of the reasons I always feel so baffled by the barrage of questions.) No, I share this anecdote because I think that whether or not you're a parent, you likely will have had this experience of abandoning your intuition in favour of somebody else's advice or guidance.

Over the years, I've seen a pattern emerge with my coaching clients, one that has also been present in my own life. They identify a change they'd like to make in their lives and then they start to look for guidance that will help them. They might head to the internet to search for knowledge, or perhaps they turn to friends, mentors, or colleagues to seek their advice. They may even invest in a course or a book. Once they've gathered advice, they then try to implement whatever information they were able to find into their own life, without making any considerations as to whether it's the right plan or approach for them, before ultimately failing to make the change and feeling despondent and self-critical as a result.

Let me share an example. A client of mine, Steph, had a goal of improving her fitness. She followed a fitness influencer on Instagram who was running an exercise challenge that involved completing a number of different workouts a week. Participating in this challenge felt like a no-brainer to Steph. Not only would it help her achieve her goal of feeling fitter, but having a plan meant she didn't need to think too much about what she was going to do and when, saving her time, which was important given that she had a busy job working for a charity. So, Steph embarked on the challenge, but within just a week or so, she was finding it hard. The workouts required a lot of equipment, which meant they needed to be completed in the gym, and given that Steph already worked long days in the office, she sometimes wasn't getting home until ten p.m. She was exhausted and struggling to find time to see friends and keep on top of her domestic duties, but as someone who strongly identifies with the perfectionist archetype, she also struggled to miss a workout or give up on the challenge. Eventually, her body gave up for her, and she ended up bedbound with a nasty bout of flu. She had assumed that following someone's else's plan would save her time and energy, but the opposite had been true—by not tuning into her own needs and schedule, she'd found herself back at square one. Once she'd made a full recovery, Steph and I were able to figure out a plan that felt more sustainable for her in the long run, one that took into consideration factors like her work commitments and what she'd enjoy most.

I worked with another client last year, Emma, who was in the process of building her own yoga business. She'd identified that in order to get more bookings for her classes, she needed to do more marketing, and she had turned to Google to help her figure out where to start. As a self-confessed procrastinator, Emma found the barrage of information completely overwhelming and ended up caught in a cycle of procrastinating by trying to find the right marketing plan for her, investing in a course or product that promised to help her, struggling to take the action outlined by said course or product, and then finding herself back on Google, hoping that the next investment would be the thing to help. What actually helped Emma was realising that she already had the resources and skills she needed to find more students for her classes. She had a great local network, and with a few conversations and some advertising in popular cafés and shops near her studio, she was able to fill her classes via word of mouth. Again, Emma had believed that turning to someone else's plan would make running her business easier, but all it had done was create more overwhelm and obstacles.

At first glance, seeking external guidance to help us make the changes we want to make doesn't seem like a terrible plan. It's reasonable to think that Steph's following a challenge, or Emma's taking part in a marketing course, or my reading about the perfect baby routine would make us more productive in achieving our desired goals. But the issue with this approach is that when we give complete power to that external guidance or information, ignoring our own intuition and instincts in the process, we often end up expending energy on actions that move us no further along, damaging our confidence in our abilities.

If we want to get more done in a way that both feels joyful and maximises efficiency, if we want to start making decisions that feel aligned with our own individual definition of success, we need to start inviting our intuition to the party.

What Is Intuition and Why Is It Important for Productivity?

The Cambridge Dictionary defines intuition as "an ability to understand or know something immediately based on your feelings rather than facts." Intuition can often seem fluffy or woo-woo, especially when held up against a more rigorous analytical approach to decision-making. However, research suggests that there is an in-depth cognitive process at play, with past experiences, cumulative knowledge, and cues from our environment all being drawn on to help us reach a rapid decision. It's thought that our intuitive processes were an essential part of human survival, helping us sense when danger might be present and make rapid and unconscious decisions when necessary. Our intuitive thoughts are not irrational or random. They are the cumulation of all the experiences we've had and the knowledge we've acquired throughout our lives.

There are lots of reasons why we might struggle to hear or trust our intuition, particularly as women. Firstly, we live in a society that values logic and data over emotion, and trusting a gut instinct over a reasoned argument can often be seen as a weakness.

However, research suggests that intuitive processing is quicker than analytical reasoning and can often be just as or even more accurate, helping us make better judgements or decisions with less energetic output. One study, conducted by experts in organisational psychology, found that this is especially likely to be the case if we already have what's referred to as *domain expertise*, which essentially means having prior knowledge and expertise in the area where we're trying to make a decision (Dane 2012). Put simply—if you have a decent amount of prior knowledge, taking an intuitive approach might help you be more productive. This seems to be the case for doctors, with one 2004 study published in the BMJ finding that a doctor's gut feeling that something was wrong when treating a child was more important for diagnosis than most signs or symptoms.

Further research suggests that women may be better suited than men to use intuition to enhance their decision-making (Bao et al. 2022), with studies showing that women are more sensitive to subtle cues and tend to demonstrate greater levels of empathy and emotional intelligence (Fischer, Kret, and Broekens 2018), all of which can benefit the intuitive process. And yet despite evidence showing that us women have high levels of intuition and that using it can help us make better decisions, we often still encounter prejudices in the workplace. I saw this a lot in my previous career: when men made intuitive decisions, they were labelled as wise and quick-thinking, whereas when women used gut feelings to help them make choices, they were described as impulsive or accused of being too driven by their emotions.

Interestingly, there is research to suggest that trying to explain our judgements with logic and reason can interrupt our intuitive processes and cause us to reach less accurate or efficient judgements (Ambady 2010). You might have had this experience before when trying to explain a decision to someone else. You start the conversation feeling confident and sure of your choice, but after trying to defend it or explain it, your confidence dips. That's because you've interrupted the intuitive process. A lack of confidence can also make it difficult to trust our instincts. Yet as we've seen in the anecdotes shared earlier in this chapter, outsourcing our decision-making to others or trying and failing to implement someone else's plan only decreases our self-confidence further.

It might feel uncomfortable to trust your intuition to begin with, particularly if you have been exposed to cultures, industries, or environments that favour logic over emotion. This has certainly been my experience. Having studied economics for my undergraduate degree and worked in large corporations and tech start-ups, I found it had been drummed into me that data was key and that every decision needed to be evidence-based and strategic. For that reason, I was sceptical of coaching as a tool and industry for a long time, suspicious that a mode that relied so much on intuition and emotional reasoning could hold value that more academic or data-based tools couldn't provide more effectively. The irony is that when I started working with a coach and nurturing my own intuition, my confidence and self-belief started to grow significantly, and I was able to show up for my dreams and ambitions more effectively.

One final block to using our intuition is being able to connect to it in the first place. When our lives are so busy and the mental load is so heavy, it can feel impossible to even tune into our inner voice and figure out what our intuition is trying to tell us. But the busier we are, the more we can benefit from using intuitive processing to help us make decisions, given that it is quicker than analytical reasoning. This is something I've certainly experienced in the last year. Prior to having my daughter, I liked to spend a lot of time researching every single decision in my business. I could lose hours weighing up different pieces of software, and whole days thinking through every element of my strategy. But once I became a parent, my time was dramatically squeezed, and nowadays, I find myself having to take a more intuitive approach. What's interesting is that my business hasn't suffered as a result—if anything, the opposite has been true. I've made better decisions, and I've also had more fun, as my time has been spent focusing on the work I love instead of endlessly researching or weighing up pros and cons. Relying more on my own intuition to make decisions has also helped me break free from the comparison trap, meaning I waste less time worrying that I'm falling behind my peers.

Of course, there are times when we need external knowledge, information, or perspectives to help us make a good decision, but it's clear that most of us would benefit from learning to listen to ourselves more if we want to not only be more productive but also make decisions that serve us better in the long run. As I often say to my clients: You know yourself better than anybody else in the world. You're the only person who has been there for every experience in your life, the only one who has felt every feeling. It's you who has learnt the lesson from every failure you've ever had. It's you who can understand what it took to create the successes. Sure, there might be people out there who can provide a bit of technical guidance or plug some knowledge gaps for you, but you are the expert in you. I've seen firsthand in my coaching practice that when women start trusting themselves, magic unfolds. What would be possible for you if you stopped endlessly researching or justifying your decisions and instead poured that energy into taking action?

LET IT GO

Consider where in your life you are most likely to seek external advice or guidance. What decisions do you find yourself running past friends and family? What situations leave you turning to Google? How might your life be different if you relied less on external noise and more on your own intuition and instincts?

What experiences in your life might have influenced the relationship you have (or don't have) with your intuition? What have you been led to believe about trusting your gut feelings? Are there any beliefs that you'd like to consciously let go of?

A Note on Boundaries and Intuition

We're going to explore boundaries in much greater detail in Chapter Eight, but for now, let's touch on how intuition can be a useful and important tool when figuring out the boundaries we need to set to protect our time and energy.

Have you ever said yes to a project or social commitment that you wished you'd said no to? I imagine the answer to that question is probably yes. As women, we are prone to overcommitting ourselves, something that, as we've discussed, can lead us further away from our own definition of success and hamper our well-being in the process. There are many reasons we might do this, including being conditioned to put the needs of others ahead of our own or simply wanting to avoid any potential confrontation. But often, when saying yes or agreeing to do something, we are ignoring our intuition.

Let me give you an example. My client Anisha was invited to take a trip with some of her friends. Her gut reaction when she read the invite in the WhatsApp chat was one of dread—there were lots of lively activities planned, and as an introvert Anisha knew she would struggle to keep pace. She also knew that she had other financial priorities, including paying off some debt she had acquired. And yet despite that strong intuitive response, she talked herself into going along anyway, reasoning that it would be rude to turn down the offer and that she would figure out a way to budget for it. As the trip grew closer, the amount of dread Anisha felt increased. It wasn't that she didn't want to spend time with friends; it was just that she knew this wasn't the forum she wanted to do it in. In a bid to make everyone else happy, she had ended up making herself feel anxious and overwhelmed, and she'd fallen behind on her goal to pay off her debt and to become more financially secure.

You might have had a similar experience to Anisha. Perhaps you've said yes to helping with a project at your kid's school, even though you knew it would eat into your much-needed downtime. Maybe you've agreed to host Christmas, even though your intuition was telling you that you'd have preferred a more low-key celebration that year. We are so adept at ignoring our intuition to please others that sometimes we don't even realise that's what we've been doing until we pause and reflect. But our intuition is a powerful tool, and ignoring it won't help us build the joyful lives we're craving; rather, it simply kicks the can down the road, giving us another problem to deal with later down the line.

We'll dive deeper into how to set and communicate boundaries later in the book, but for now, when you're making plans or responding to invites, try to notice what your intuition is telling you. If something doesn't feel good to you when you agree to it, the chances are that it's not going to feel good when the time rolls around. Trusting our intuition might just be the greatest act of self-care.

Productivity Archetypes and Intuition

How do we start to tap into our knowledge or expertise for guidance? How do we tune into our intuition? How do we know if the gut feeling we're experiencing is our intuition or anxiety? How do we learn to trust our instincts in a society that seems to favour data and rigour over feelings and emotions?

These are all questions I've been asked by my clients over the years, and if I'm honest, they're questions I sometimes come back to myself, despite knowing all the research. I've found that the best way to tune into and start to trust our own intuition and knowledge varies depending on our productivity archetype, and so I want to explore each one in turn.

The Doer

If you identify as a doer, the biggest challenge to trusting your intuition and instincts is having the time and space to hear and engage with them. Doers often notice that it's only when they take a step back from their usual life, during a vacation or the holidays for example, that they're able to tune into their inner voice. That's what happened to me. I identify as a doer, especially when it comes to career, and before I did the work to carve out time to connect with my intuition, I'd often have these big revelations when I was taking a trip. Take our honeymoon in 2018, for example. I'd long had a niggling feeling that my current career wasn't right for me, but it was only when I broke out of my routine for three weeks and flew over five thousand miles away that I was able to fully hear my intuition and see that I was spending all my energy building a career that wasn't serving me or my values. I can remember sitting in a bar in Portland, Oregon, in a completely different time zone from my colleagues and loved ones, and realising that if I wanted anything to change, I needed to redirect that energy into building something new. I booked a call with a coach for the week we were due to arrive home, and I never looked back.

While of course as women our to-do lists are already very long, I've noticed that doers often add more to the list (consciously or subconsciously) in order to distract themselves from the voice in their head. This particularly seems to be the case if it's trying to share an inconvenient truth with us that will require us to make a change in some way. But it's vital to accept that by not carving out time to connect and engage with our intuition, we risk driving ourselves further down a path that isn't right for us and creating more work for our future selves. We can't build a more joyful and intentional future for ourselves if we're never still enough to decipher what that will look and feel like.

✸ *Try* **This** ✸

Create time in your schedule to engage with your intuition. Here are some ideas of how you might do that:

- Start a journaling practice. Something that has really helped me is freewriting two to three pages in my journal each day, not following any prompt or agenda, and simply noticing whatever shows up when I put pen to paper. Often, there's a thought or niggling feeling lurking that I would have otherwise missed. If you feel like you need a prompt to get you started, you can begin by writing "Today I feel . . ." and see what shows up for you. And if writing isn't your thing, why not record a voice note? You don't have to send it to anyone, but simply taking a moment to check in with and process your thoughts will provide clarity.
- Break up the busyness. Doers can often live on autopilot, rushing from one thing to the next with no time to think. A great way to reconnect with your intuition is by consciously breaking up the busyness—taking a walk around the block at lunchtime, for example, or keeping one evening free a week to simply putter. Scheduling more regular downtime may also help quiet your busy brain—sometimes doers can find that even when they're not doing something, they can still be analysing, planning, or worrying. The better you can get at quieting your mind, the easier it will be to tune into your intuition.
- Take a mindful moment. One last tip that helps me is to identify something that you do several times a day, and use that activity as a way to check in with how you're feeling. Because I'm a British stereotype who drinks a lot of tea, I like to pause and notice how my day is going when my cup is brewing, but perhaps you could check in at mealtimes or when you take a bathroom break. It doesn't have to be formal or detailed—it's more about getting into the habit of interrupting your thoughts at multiple points throughout the day.

The Perfectionist

If you identify as a perfectionist, you might have a similar challenge to my client Steph, whose experience I shared earlier, where your drive to do something "perfectly" means it's hard to listen to your intuition or instincts if doing so will make you feel that you've failed in some way. Additionally, your desire for perfection might have made you believe that there is a "right" way of doing something, an attitude that gets in the way of your ability to be creative or innovative. For example, my client Laura was so keen to get things right and to perform perfectly at work that she followed her boss's instructions to the letter, ignoring her intuition when it told her there was a better way of completing the project. By not listening to her intuition, Laura failed to spot an opportunity that her colleague seized on, meaning she came across as less smart and observant. Not only was this frustrating, but it also meant that she was passed over in favour for her colleague next time a promotion came along.

Just as doers keep themselves busy to avoid listening to their intuition, perfectionists subscribe to the idea of a "perfect" way of doing something for the same reason. It can feel even more powerful, given that our idea about what makes something "perfect" is so heavily influenced by our parents, our peers, and wider society. But it's important to try to invite some flexibility into your thinking and remember that there is no one perfect way of completing a task or living a life. Just like there is no one perfect way of being a great daughter or sister or mother or friend. There is only the way that feels good to you and allows you to thrive.

Try This

Next time you need to make a change, instead of searching for the perfect plan, try the experiment approach:

Step 1: Identify the desired change you want to make.

Step 2: Brainstorm the most joyful ways you could make this change.

Step 3: Plan and execute an experiment around one of your joyful ideas.

Step 4: Reflect and learn—was your hypothesis correct? What have you learnt for your next experiment?

What I love about this approach, and why it works so well for perfectionists, is that you can't fail at an experiment—you can only learn something new. Say you have an idea that working out every day will make you feel good. You try it out for a week and realise that, actually, while you enjoyed some of the workouts, you feel exhausted and have struggled to make time for your other priorities. This realisation doesn't mean your experiment has failed—far from it. You've had a go at something, have learnt from the experience, and now have some really valuable information to help you plan a better experiment next time. Taking this approach also gives you a permission slip to quit if something isn't working, which can help you avoid the danger of staying on the wrong path for too long—something that can be incredibly detrimental to not only our productivity but also our overall sense of well-being and life satisfaction.

You might like to invite friends, colleagues, or loved ones to help you during Step Two—having a few different perspectives will remind you that there's no one perfect approach.

The Dreamer

Dreamers tend to have the best relationships with their intuition and instincts of all the productivity archetypes, but their biggest challenge is that they might not realise it! One of my long-standing clients, Chloe, is a classic dreamer. She can tell you in great detail about the sort of life she'd like to live, and she gets very strong gut instincts about what to say yes or no to. Her trouble is that she struggles to take action based on those gut instincts because she has been told time and again throughout her life that she needs to be more realistic in her planning. This in turn creates a feeling of resentment when she sees other people living out the dreams she has for herself while she's struggling to give herself permission to just go for it. The focus of our work together has been in accepting that her dreams are not something reserved for thinking about on her commute but rather strong guides from her intuition about what she should be prioritising or seeking in her life. And in doing that, she has been able to show up and take action, spending three months travelling and finally applying for the PhD programme that had long been sitting on her one-day list.

If you identify with Chloe, maybe it's time for you to start doing the same. Telling yourself that dreams are simply dreams might feel like the safer option, because in not taking action to make them come true, you don't risk failing at achieving them. However, not taking action is a failure in and of itself and will only lead to resentment and disappointment. And here's the thing: those people who may have told you that your dreams are unrealistic don't really have any idea of what is realistic for you. The chances are that their comments were simply a projection of their own biases, fears, or insecurities, as opposed to a useful judgement about you. The only way you'll achieve your definition of success is by showing up for it. It's time to start doing just that.

✸ *Try* This ✸

A top tip if you struggle with believing that your dreams are "realistic" is to find evidence that making them come true is possible. There are very few things that you could dream up that would be truly impossible for you to bring to life, and realising this can help you start taking action. Here are some ways you might do that:

- Whatever your intuition is telling you to do, find someone who has already walked that path—whether it's a person you know in real life or someone you can follow on social media or listen to on a podcast. Being able to see that someone has already made this change, particularly if their circumstances are similar to yours, will challenge your perspective. It might also be useful to look for women's networks in your area who can support you and cheer you on.
- Think about the tools and resources you have available to you. When Chloe and I started exploring applying for her PhD programme, she realised that she had a few contacts who could help guide her through the process and that her previous experience working at university would help. Sometimes, you don't realise how well equipped you are until you face the change head-on and start creating a plan.
- Write a list of things that have previously felt like pipe dreams that are now your reality. Nelson Mandela's "It always seems impossible until it's done" quote is popular for a reason—change can feel hard, but that doesn't mean it's not worth pursuing.

The Procrastinator

In my experience, procrastinators feel more aligned with dreamers in that their biggest challenge isn't hearing their intuition but instead taking action based on it. In fact, procrastinators are veritable experts in avoiding taking action on their gut instincts! Let me tell you about my client Carmel. Carmel had built a strong public sector career, but she had always had a feeling that she wasn't on the right path and that she would thrive more working in a creative field. She sought out coaching with me to help her make this change, and we set out to do just that. By the end of every call, Carmel would be feeling certain that this career change was right for her and would have a list of actions that she was going to take to get the ball rolling, but whenever we got together for our next call, she would be no further along in the process. It took us a few sessions to realise that what was happening in between our calls was that logic was creeping in and interrupting the intuitive process, making it difficult for Carmel to show up for the action that she wanted to take.

Together, we figured out that Carmel needed to close the gap between having an intuitive thought and taking action, reducing the exposure to analytical thinking and other people's opinions that would set her offtrack. She started blocking out the few hours after our coaching calls to take action, and within a few months, Carmel had completed a graphic design course and landed her first freelance client.

When you have an intuitive thought, take action on it, even if it's tiny. For example, perhaps you have a strong pull to visit Italy. When you experience that pull, spend a few minutes researching specific destinations or flight costs. Then, take the next step as soon as you can. Notice how it feels to show up for your dream, even in a tiny way, and then identify the next step and repeat the process.

The idea is to keep the process intuitive and not get lost in the overwhelm of creating a big plan. By focusing on the action, you'll spend less time and energy worrying about whether it's the right thing to do and more time and energy moving in the direction of your dreams.

DO IT YOUR WAY

Identify a time when you have trusted your intuition in the past and it has helped you make a positive change in your life. What helped you tune into your intuition and trust that it was right in that scenario? Is there anything you can learn from that experience?

It might also be useful to consider a time when you didn't trust your intuition, and what you can learn from that scenario. Remember to tread gently: approaching with compassion and curiosity will serve you better than using this as an opportunity to judge or beat yourself up.

Some Other Tools to Help You Get in Touch with Your Intuition

Before we wrap up this chapter, I want to share a few other tools or rituals that can help you get in touch with and deepen your relationship with your intuition.

1. Use tarot or oracle cards

One way to tap into your intuition is to pull a tarot or oracle card and notice your reaction to it or explore how it applies to a situation that you're in. Start by thinking about a decision or situation in your life that you feel like you need some guidance on, then pull a card from the deck. (You can also find free oracle or tarot card generators online if you'd like to try this but don't have a deck.) Reflect on what your chosen card means and notice how you feel when considering it in relation to your situation or decision.

It may be that you feel like the card offers up validation of your intuitive thoughts, or you might feel strongly that the meaning of it isn't useful—either way, you'll be engaging with your intuition and noticing what does or doesn't feel true and meaningful to you.

2. Tune into your body

In our busy, fast-paced world, the wisdom of our bodies is often underutilised. Tuning into our bodies and how they react to certain ideas can be a great way of reconnecting with our intuition. The following steps can help you do just that:

- Consider a decision, big or small, that you need to make. For example, perhaps you need to decide whether to apply for a promotion at work.
- Think about the different options you have available to you. So, using our example, your options might be: apply for the promotion, speak to HR to find out more about the promotion, or stay in your current position.
- Then, take each option in turn and picture yourself living that decision. Pay close attention to how your body reacts. Do you feel tense or light when you imagine this reality? What happens in your stomach? How does your breathing change?
- When you're imagining the most intuitive decision for you, you will probably notice that your body language feels more open and you feel a little lighter. There might still be some activity in your stomach, but it will feel more like butterflies than a churning knot.

3. Connect with your wise future self

The final tool I want to share with you is all about connecting with your wise future self. It's often easier for us to access our intuition when we zoom out of any immediate threats, fears, or challenges and instead focus on the big picture.

Start by picturing your wise future self. Imagine that they have lived through all the challenges of your life and have reached old age feeling content and joyful. Spend a few minutes trying to embody this future self, before writing a letter from them to current you. Consider what advice they might have for you—what do they think it's important for you to know in this season of life?

I hope you are starting to see that your intuition is not something to be dismissed; it's your most powerful guide. You know yourself better than anybody else in the world. Of course you do! The fact that you or I ever doubt this shows just how hard our systems and structures have worked to foster that doubt.

Because when we doubt ourselves, we are pliable. We are more easily marketed to. We are more likely to buy the things we don't need. We stay later at the office. We spend more time scrolling. We give our attention and time and money away freely. We make decisions that don't align with our values. We relinquish our power more easily.

Learning to listen to and trust our intuition is how we take our power back. It's a radical act, one that won't just save you a lot of time and energy, making you more productive, but will also build a deep sense of knowing and confidence that you will carry with you for life. That's pretty vital work if you ask me.

LET'S RECAP

- Many of us outsource our decision-making and planning to others that we believe are better qualified, but in doing so, we often ignore our intuition and end up making decisions that don't move us forwards or align with our definition of success.
- Research has shown that trusting our intuition can help us make quicker and more accurate judgements, particularly if we already have expertise in the area, helping us be more productive. Women are thought to be more intuitive, but we also face more blocks to connecting with and trusting our intuition, with strong biases for more traditionally masculine traits, such as data analysis, prevailing.
- Our relationship with our intuition may vary depending on our productivity archetype:
    - Doers and perfectionists, to avoid listening to their intuition, like to keep themselves busy or subscribe to the idea that there is a "perfect" way.
    - Conversely, dreamers and procrastinators are often better at hearing their intuition but struggle to trust or act on the downloads they receive.
    - You can start to build a better relationship with your intuition by identifying one area of life you can tune in to more using the activities or exercises outlined in this chapter. Remember that this is a process—the skill of intuitive thinking can be built with practise over time.

CHAPTER 7:

PLAY TO YOUR STRENGTHS

I've been given a lot of advice throughout my career, but there's one particular piece that still sticks with me almost fifteen years after I received it. It's guidance that I've come back to so many times over the last decade and a half, and one that I've shared with many friends and clients too. In fact, now that I think about it, this piece of advice also forms the basis of one of the key pillars of my signature career-change programme, Find Your Thing.

The advice—to play to my strengths—was given to me during the first year of my graduate scheme, which I completed at a large international corporate organisation. For the uninitiated, a graduate scheme is kind of like a training programme for recent graduates. Organisations take on young, driven individuals and offer them exposure to different areas of the business, alongside lots of training and development, with the understanding being that the individuals will be able to offer new perspectives and add more value as a result of the scheme. The graduate scheme I completed was set up brilliantly, and I had lots of access to learning and development opportunities. One of the big perks was getting matched with a mentor who held a position of seniority in the business, and for that first year of my graduate scheme, I was matched with the company sales director, a man who was really friendly and personable but who intimidated me all the same.

It was my first real experience of mentoring, at least in any formal capacity. The learning-and-development team had set up an initial meeting for us, and it was up to me to prepare topics for discussion. My fellow graduates and I had recently been through a competency-analysis exercise, outlining our natural strengths and weaknesses, and I thought it would be great to start by reviewing each of my weaknesses. Then I could ask my mentor for advice on how to plug the gaps in my skill set.

We sat down for a coffee, and I plunged straight in, nervously babbling away about what the exercise had revealed about my weaknesses and the ideas I had to try to fix them.

"Can I just stop you there?" asked my mentor. "Why are you choosing to fix your weaknesses instead of building on your strengths?"

He then went on to tell me that all the most successful people he knew had flaws aplenty, and they weren't wasting any time trying to correct them. Instead, they were focusing on the stuff they were really good at and using that to get ahead. My mentor even generously went on to list some of his own weaknesses to prove his point, highlighting that he struggled with creativity and was pretty terrible at administrative tasks.

I was quite literally stunned by his advice. I can remember sitting there, stopped in my tracks and stumbling over my words, not quite sure what to say in response. Because this idea, of prioritising my strengths and letting go of the need to fix my weaknesses, was in direct opposition to everything I'd ever been told about success and productivity.

At school, it was the well-rounded who were celebrated, and I worked my backside off to make sure I fit into that category. I was praised for doing just as well in art as I did in mathematics and was even elected as my school's head girl (the most senior student-leadership role you can attain) for my ability to juggle extracurricular activities with my academic studies. What I internalised from my time at school was that I had to be able to do it all in order to be a success. My university and early career experiences only seemed to back that belief up—I was endlessly encouraged to pursue a variety of opportunities to bolster my experience and develop my weaknesses. And yet here was someone who was undeniably very successful telling me that to succeed I needed to focus on my strengths, not my weaknesses.

I felt as if I were being let in on a huge secret. I'll be honest—sometimes I still feel that way. Because I know, from the work I do as a consultant and coach, that so many of us, and us women particularly, are still subscribing to the idea that we need to be good at everything to get ahead. We push ourselves to be more productive because we believe that not only should we be doing it all, but we should be doing it all well. We sacrifice our already-squeezed time so that we don't appear weak or inadequate. We stay silent in meetings or hold back from applying for promotions out of fear that we'll expose ourselves in some way.

And it's easy to understand why—we exist in a world where our popularity and likeability still go some way to determining our levels of success, especially for those who belong to a marginalised group. Yet research has shown that if women display traits that are typically deemed "masculine," such as assertiveness or strong leadership skills, this could make them appear less kind or nurturing, which in turn lowers their likeability score (Seo 2023). With so many expectations placed on women, it's little wonder that we are challenging ourselves to fit the mould, yet these impossible double standards demonstrate that no matter how hard we hustle, it's never quite enough. What would happen if we stopped trying to be great at everything and instead focused on simply supercharging our strengths? What would happen if we embraced who we are rather than tried to pretend we're someone we're not? Well, it would seem from the research in the field of positive psychology that quite a lot would change for the better.

Studies have shown that focusing on our strengths helps build greater well-being, reduce the amount of stress we experience, and improve our vitality (Wood et al. 2011). Further research from Gallup (n.d.) has shown that when we know what our strengths are, we are able to form better partnerships, improving our ability to work in team settings. But the real clincher? Knowing and using our strengths regularly is correlated with greater productivity. In fact, analysis from Gallup (2015) revealed that people who use their strengths every day are six times more likely to be engaged at work and are at least 8 percent more productive than their peers. There's no getting away from the fact that using our strengths is key for mastering sustained performance. Researchers in the field of positive psychology theorise that this is because using our strengths builds tenacity, reduces stress, and increases adaptability, making it easier to persevere with our goals—but also because it requires less willpower to keep doing things that we enjoy.

I had this experience when I was studying for my master's programme in psychology. The work was of course challenging, and adding on a full-time degree to an already-busy life meant that I was juggling a lot. But the programme felt very aligned with my strengths of curiosity, intrapersonal skills, and communication, which meant that I was energised, motivated, and able to tackle my studies efficiently. This was such a different experience from studying for my undergraduate degree in economics, when I regularly felt like I was having to battle my weaknesses just to keep up. To me, leaning into and using my strengths feels like flowing with the tide and letting it carry me forwards instead of fighting to resist it.

Knowing and understanding our strengths can also help us set more joyful goals for ourselves. When we understand where our strengths lie, we are more likely to set goals that mean something to us and that move us closer to our authentic definition of success. Plus, when we start setting goals that are about supercharging our strengths instead of trying to fix weaknesses, we're much more likely to enjoy the process of pursuing those goals.

For example, my client Heather had a goal of buying her first home. Heather was in her mid-thirties, and many of her friends had already got on the property ladder, but as much as she craved the security and comfort of having a place of her own, the process of getting there felt completely overwhelming to her. As a result, she kept putting off getting started, clinging to any potential obstacles as a reason to push the goal further down the to-do list, until years had passed and she realised she hadn't made any material progress.

One of the biggest things that overwhelmed Heather was that she felt like the process of buying her first home would require her to overcome her weaknesses. She had been told in the past that she wasn't very organised, and she struggled with numbers and detailed admin. The thought of having to manage the process and talk about her finances with a mortgage broker felt like hard and uncomfortable work, and so instead she procrastinated. When we started working together, one of the first things we did was identify Heather's strengths and look at how she could use these to help her achieve her goal. Her strength of creativity, for example, allowed her to see past poor decor, meaning she was well placed to spot a bargain, and she was also very skilled at bringing people together who could help her. By focusing on these strengths instead of becoming overwhelmed by her perceived weaknesses, Heather was able to find both a new home and also the right legal and financial professionals to help her manage the process.

When we approach our goals through the lens of our strengths, new perspectives and ideas open up to us. We feel more confident and are better able to enjoy the process too. Plus, we often realise that we don't need to do it all alone, which can feel very freeing. It seems that my mentor of fifteen years ago was onto something.

LET IT GO

Humans are biased towards negativity, a hangover from our hunter-gatherer days when spotting risks was essential for survival. This bias can be stronger in women, given the risks and barriers we face. However, focusing too much on our weaknesses can hurt our confidence and productivity, leading us to pursue activities misaligned with our definitions of success and well-being. Try to identify a weakness you no longer desire to fix and consider how accepting it might change your life.

For example, organisation is one of my weaknesses. For years, I have invested time, energy, and money into trying to become more organised, spending entire weekends reorganising my closet and a small fortune trying to find the perfect day planner that would keep me focused. I've now accepted that organisation is never going to be a strength of mine, and where it's important for me to have a greater sense of order—for example, managing the finances and taxes for my business—I outsource the task to someone who has being organised as a strength. By accepting this weakness and letting go of trying to fix it, I've been able to free up more time to focus on the things I am great at and enjoy, which has helped me be more productive.

Outsourcing or asking for help can be challenging for women, particularly if we have been raised in cultures or environments in which being able to manage it all ourselves is seen as a badge of honour, and sometimes we try to persevere with our weaknesses for this reason. This was the case for my client Leela. In her culture, caring for the home was an important part of being a "good" wife, yet she found it difficult to keep on top of domestic duties. Initially, hiring some help felt to Leela like both a betrayal of her roots and an acceptance that she had failed as a wife. However, a few months in, her perspective changed. She felt much more relaxed and able to be present for her work and her relationship, and she also felt good that she was able to support the business of a local professional too.

Accepting our weaknesses and working around them might feel uncomfortable to begin with, but some short-term discomfort is surely better than a lifetime of trying to push against a tide.

Identifying and Supercharging Your Strengths

So, we know that using our strengths can help us be more productive, but how do we go about identifying what they are? There are a few questions and exercises that I like to use with my clients to get them thinking about where their natural strengths lie. You could block out some time to explore these prompts in your journal, get together to discuss them with friends, or simply reflect on them in the coming days.

- What tasks or activities give you energy?
- What would you like to do more of and why?
- What were you good at or what did you enjoy as a child?
- What roles do you tend to slip into? For example, are you the organised one who always plans the social events, or the good listener who everyone comes to with their problems?
- What positive feedback do you regularly receive? What qualities are you often praised for?
- Text or email a few people in your life and ask them to describe you in five words. Aim for a cross section of your life when you're reaching out to people. For example, a colleague, a close loved one, a friend, etc.
- Write down what you do each day, including tasks from both your personal and professional life. Highlight the tasks that come most naturally to you. What can they tell you about your strengths?

Once you've explored these questions and exercises, write down a list of your strengths. It can sometimes feel uncomfortable to see our strengths written down, particularly if we have been raised to believe that humility is important, as many women have. But identifying them is the first step to owning them.

The next step is to consider how you can put your strengths into action more. This is important because it's using them that gives us those benefits I described earlier, not just knowing them.

Again, I know that this can feel difficult to do, particularly if it's a novel idea or something you haven't given much thought to before. A task that can help is to go through each strength in turn and jot down one or two ways that you could use it more in your everyday life to be more joyful—and ultimately more productive. Think about both your personal and professional life here and allow yourself to get creative. Here are some examples:

- If you have a strength of creativity, perhaps you could challenge yourself to come up with multiple solutions to a problem before deciding on the most impactful one, or experiment with presenting information in a new way. Additionally, you could get your creative juices flowing at home by rearranging one of the rooms in your home or experimenting with a new journaling prompt. Finally, perhaps you could work on a new creative project, whether that be writing a story or painting something beautiful—using your creativity isn't just about engaging with the arts, but there's no reason why it can't be!
- If you have a strength of curiosity, perhaps you could meet someone from a different work team for a coffee and find out more about what they do, or read a book or listen to a podcast about something you've always been interested in. You could even just head out for a walk around your neighbourhood, paying attention to what is going on around you and trying to see your local area through fresh eyes.
- If you have a strength of leadership, perhaps you could share words of encouragement with others and help them see the value they add, or maybe you could volunteer to lead a new project at your kid's school. You could even take the lead on organising your next family gathering, setting the vision for the event and engaging with other members of the family to help you bring it to life.

The aim here is to simply get into the habit of connecting with your strengths and giving yourself permission to focus on supercharging them instead of fixing your weaknesses.

Over time, you might notice that by focusing on using your strengths, you start to feel both more joyful and more productive. I've seen this play out time and again with my clients, and I notice it in my own life too. Just a few weeks ago, I was feeling overwhelmed and like I was heading for a minor episode of burnout. I took some time to reconnect with my strengths and to think about how I could put them into action more, noticing that a few of them, such as gratitude and connection, were underused. My negativity bias told me that writing a gratitude list or calling a friend weren't big enough actions to change how I was feeling, but thankfully my understanding of the science gave me the motivation I needed to do it anyway. Within a few days of engaging with those strengths, I felt more energised and like the best and most authentic version of myself.

As mentioned earlier, societal and cultural expectations might make the task of identifying and owning your strengths feel like more of a struggle. It may be useful to think about how gendered expectations might have shaped your perception of your strengths and weaknesses over time. For example, perhaps you have held back from truly owning your strength of leadership because you've been so aware of the backlash and double standards that female leaders face. Or perhaps you have felt shame around fully embracing your strength of empathy because you've worked in an environment where technical skills were valued far more favourably than interpersonal skills. Or maybe you've failed to spot your strengths because they've always been spoken about as weaknesses by someone else. For example, maybe you've been reprimanded for socialising too much at work instead of being celebrated for your ability to gel with other teams, or maybe your love of arts and crafts was always framed as a hobby that was less important than your academic studies instead of as a sign of your creativity.

In my experience, once you can see how your perception of your strengths has been shaped by external forces, it's easier to come home to what feels most true to you. Embracing our true strengths and allowing ourselves to accept who we are rather than striving to be someone different is not just a better use of our energy; it is a loving act of self-care that supports our well-being and self-esteem.

Try This

If you'd like a little more help identifying what your strengths are, a great tool is the VIA Character Strengths survey. Developed by positive psychology heavyweights Dr. Christopher Peterson and Dr. Martin Seligman (2004), the Character Strengths survey will help you identify the positive parts of your personality that make you feel most authentic and engaged. What I like about this survey is the emphasis that you possess all the twenty-four character strengths covered but that you will have a preference for some more than others, creating your unique strengths profile. The aim is to simply notice what comes most naturally to you so you can take advantage of those qualities and skills.

You can find the survey here: https://www.viacharacter.org.

Productivity Archetypes and Strengths

Before I leave you to think about identifying your strengths, I want to explore how your relationship with your strengths might differ depending on your productivity archetype and share some tips and watch-outs that might help you use your strengths more.

The Doer

Doers are generally tenacious and driven, and their biggest watch-out when it comes to using their strengths is falling victim to the idea that if something is hard to do, it's more worthwhile. This is a trap I've fallen into myself many times. I grew up hearing the phrases *nothing worth having comes easy* and *if it were easy, everybody would be doing it*, and I internalised these to mean that the things that come naturally to me are somehow less worthwhile. But that simply isn't the case. When you're good at something, you can add more value in the same amount of time as you can working at something that doesn't come naturally to you, and you will also find it easier to keep showing up over a sustained period of time.

This realisation has made a huge change to how I approach things in my life. Let me share the example of maintaining my fitness. I used to think that I had to be pushing myself all the time for my efforts to be worthwhile. As a result, I would challenge myself to do something extreme, like train for a marathon or a Tough Mudder event. But I always struggled to maintain the willpower it took to do something that didn't feel natural to me, and as a result, my exercise routine was very much all or nothing. Nowadays, I lean into the things that feel easier and more enjoyable to me—going for hikes or embracing my love of swimming—and I find that it takes a lot less energy to maintain the consistency needed for me to feel good.

Another watch-out for doers is taking on tasks that don't align with their strengths, just because they feel like someone should do something. Try to resist raising your hand and volunteering yourself for another project in your next work meeting—the chances are that there will be someone better equipped to handle it, meaning that you can focus on adding value to the projects where you can truly thrive.

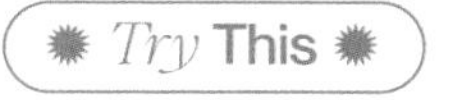

Challenge yourself to choose the "easy" option for the next week or so. Notice how it makes you feel and how it impacts your productivity. You might like to find a fellow doer to try this experiment with for extra accountability.

The Perfectionist

If you identify as a perfectionist, the chances are that you felt some resistance during the part of this chapter where I asked you to consider which weaknesses you might abandon trying to fix. In my work, I've found that perfectionists are particularly resistant to letting go of the idea that we need to be able to do it all in order to be productive or worthy, and they will often secretly harbour a belief that they will be the one to crack the formula and be a perfect all-rounder.

If that description resonates for you, perhaps this reminder can be your motivation to make a change: when you go all in on your strengths, you will become better at them than you can even imagine right now. It might feel hard to delegate to others whose strengths are better suited to a task, especially if you've spent your whole life striving to be well-rounded, but it's a much more productive approach. Let me share with you an example from my client Leanne. Leanne prided herself on being a model employee and being able to do it all, but as her capacity was squeezed, she realised she needed to make some changes. She asked a colleague to help her run some reports that would usually take her hours, and by outsourcing that task on her to-do list, she was able to spend more time on the part of her job she was great at—developing bold and impactful marketing campaigns. Freeing up that extra time gave her an edge, and her bosses soon noticed. Leanne was promoted quicker than she was expecting, and she felt more energised and engaged at work.

If you struggle with letting go of a task completely because you worry somebody else won't meet your same standards, you could consider giving at least part of it away. For example, if you get annoyed that your kids don't wash and polish the glassware as well as you do, don't let that be a reason to excuse them from helping out at all—letting them do the other 85 percent of the washing up and helping them with the glasses still gives you more time back than you doing the full job yourself.

Consider what letting go of trying to overcome your weaknesses might create time for. What can you be the best at if you stop trying to be good at everything?

The Dreamer

I've had the pleasure of supporting lots of dreamers throughout my time as a coach, and the biggest challenge they seem to face when it comes to this topic is fully seeing the potential of their strengths. Let me share with you the experience of my client Emma. Emma has all the strengths you'd imagine a dreamer to possess—she's creative, she can innovatively solve problems, and she's great at helping other people to see the big picture. The issue we ran into when we first started working together wasn't in identifying these strengths but in helping Emma to see the value in them.

You see, throughout her education and early career history, much of the feedback that Emma received was dismissive of her core strengths. She was told that she needed to focus less on her creativity and more on her academic studies and was told that she needed to get better at seeing projects through as opposed to dreaming up ideas for new ones. This all led Emma to believe that her strengths were worthless, something that couldn't be further from the truth. She also felt some shame in wanting to use her strengths, because they had been put down by others. Whenever she felt a pull to explore a new project, she could hear other people's voices in her head telling her that she lacked commitment or had her head in the clouds, all of which contributed to Emma wanting to hide her strengths away. Frustratingly, as women we are often told that our skills are frivolous or less worthy than those deemed more "masculine"—even the very fact that we call skills relating to care and communication soft skills highlights how they're perceived by society. But the truth is that we need a whole spectrum of skills in our communities in order to thrive.

Through our time working together, Emma was able to see the value she could add in different areas of her life by leaning into her strengths, and this provided a huge boost to her confidence, reducing the amount of time she spent questioning her abilities.

If you're struggling to see the value in your strengths, find someone you admire that possesses the same strengths as you. What inspires you about them? How do they use their strengths to make a positive impact on the world?

The Procrastinator

As we've discussed before, procrastinators may have a stronger negativity bias than the other productivity archetypes. This can mean that they struggle to spot their strengths and sometimes even fall into the trap of seeing their strengths as weaknesses, believing they need to make big changes before they can be the people they want to be or take the action they desire.

Let me give you an example. My client Lydia works as a copywriter for a marketing agency. We have been working together to help her take the next step in her career, and in a recent coaching call, Lydia told me she'd need to become more assertive so she could apply for more senior roles. In our discussion, she revealed that she'd once been given some feedback that she didn't speak up in meetings enough, and she had internalised that this meant she was too shy, identifying this as a weakness she needed to overcome. As we explored this together, it became clear that Lydia isn't shy or unassertive—instead, she has very strong listening skills and cares deeply about hearing what others are sharing in meetings. These are skills she has worked hard to hone as it helps her gather as much information as possible during the creative-briefing process and makes her better at her job. Being able to identify that this is a strength and not a weakness to overcome helped Lydia to realise that she is better prepared to apply for a promotion than she'd initially believed.

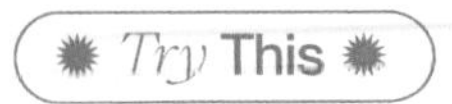

Identify three of your perceived weaknesses and challenge yourself to see them as strengths. You can see some examples below:

- If you lack attention to detail, perhaps this could mean you have a strength of generating ideas or seeing the big picture.
- If you've struggled in the past with handling conflict, perhaps this is because you have high levels of empathy.
- If you struggle to be flexible, perhaps this is because you're motivated by hitting a deadline or delivering a project on time.

As we've discussed many times in this book already, we are all different and unique. I hope that you're starting to see that this is a brilliant thing, not something to be changed or worried about. Just like we all have different definitions of success, we will all have different strengths that help us get there. Embracing those strengths is a way of celebrating our uniqueness and adding more joy to our lives.

It's time to reject the idea that some strengths are more valuable than others. It's time to let go of the idea that we need to be "perfect" and without any weaknesses in order to be happy. True fulfilment relies on your ability to accept and embrace who you are, and embracing your strengths is a vital part of that. Yes, it will make you more productive, but it will also make you happier and more confident too.

Your strengths are the things that light you up, the glorious quirks and brilliances that make you, you. When you start pouring your energy into supercharging them instead of constantly trying to fix your weaknesses, your potential is limitless.

LET'S RECAP

- Knowing and using our strengths can help us access a whole host of benefits, including increased productivity and improved well-being.
- Trying to fix our weaknesses often makes us less productive and also negatively impacts our confidence.
- As women, we face certain expectations or double standards that can make it more challenging to embrace our strengths, but letting go of what we've been taught can help us live a more joyful and fulfilling life.
- We all have different blocks that get in the way of us being able to identify and utilise our strengths, and these are often influenced by our productivity archetypes.

CHAPTER 8:

EMBRACE THE BLEND & FIND YOUR FLOW

I haven't always worked as a coach and positive psychology practitioner. In fact, as I mentioned earlier in the book, I spent the first decade of my career climbing the corporate ranks at global organisations like The Walt Disney Company. During that time, balance was elusive. Without a doubt, work was the focal point of my life, and everything else was squeezed into the margins.

I could say that this lack of balance was inevitable given the type of career I was pursuing, but I'm not sure that that's one-hundred-percent true. Sure, there were elements of my roles that caused me to devote a hefty amount of my time to work. For example, I had to travel a lot, which ate into my evenings and weekends. Also, working with colleagues in different countries meant I often needed to be available outside typical office hours. However, I'd also fallen into the trap of busyness that I wrote about in Chapter One, convincing myself that working fifty- or sixty-hour weeks and replying to emails around the clock meant that I was important, driven, and more likely to succeed. Looking back, I can see that my inclination to prioritise work above everything else was also probably influenced by the stage of life I was in. Being in my twenties meant that, first, I didn't have many other responsibilities demanding my time or focus and, second, I felt like I had something to prove.

However, working in this way for such a long period of time took its toll, and I experienced multiple bouts of burnout. When I quit my corporate career in 2019 to develop my own coaching practice, I vowed that I'd finally commit to achieving that elusive work-life balance I'd heard other people wax lyrical about. And I'll be honest, I thought that it was going to be an easy endeavour. All the things that had held me back previously—having to impress a boss, lacking control over my time, factoring in other people's deadlines and agendas—had disappeared. I had complete freedom over my new schedule and commitments. Surely dedicating an equal amount of time and energy to the professional and personal would be simple now?

Well, as I quickly found out, not quite. I started off well. I revelled in being able to start work a little later so that I could get out for a long walk each morning, and I tried to take the odd afternoon off to pick my nephew up from school, both things that I'd dreamt of being able to do while I was preparing to make the change. But within a month or two, my calendar was looking just as full as it had been in my previous jobs. I was spending long days at my desk working on the marketing and admin for my business before seeing coaching clients in the evenings and on weekend mornings. And I was finding it more difficult than ever to switch off, quickly learning that when you're building something from scratch, there's always something to be done.

I'll admit, I felt like a failure. I had intentionally set out to create a greater sense of balance in my life, and yet I'd found myself working even more than I had in my corporate roles. And that sense of failure played on me. I worried constantly about my lack of work-life balance and spent lots of time researching hacks and tips to try to make things feel more harmonious. Ironically, that was time I could have spent hanging out with my family or prioritising moments of self-care.

Then one day I met up with an old friend for a coffee. This friend is someone I've always been inspired by, but I particularly admired how she'd been able to maintain an ambitious career while also making plenty of time for her family and hobbies. But when I asked her how she was maintaining a work-life balance, she laughed. "I don't have a work-life balance," she told me. "Every week looks different. Some weeks, I don't get to leave the office until late, and on others, I'm missing meetings because my kids need me. That's life. It ebbs and flows. Balance is impossible." She then went on to explain that instead of striving for work-life balance (a goal she found just as anxiety-inducing as I did), she now embraces a work-life blend, accepting that she'll never find perfect harmony and instead showing up for whatever her biggest priority is at any given period of time.

This struck a chord with me. I was in the very early stages of starting and growing a business, so of course my work was going to require a lot from me in this season of my life. But I could see that if I kept the idea of a work-life blend front of mind, there would also be times when I could step back and be more present for my other priorities and passions. And I knew that my energy would ebb and flow too. There would be seasons when I was inspired and ready to give my work my all and times when I would feel the need to rest and retreat or fill my cup in some other way. Instead of striving for a routine or schedule that allowed me to achieve perfect balance, I softened into the idea of blending the different areas of my work and life. I accepted that the blend would look different depending on what was going on at any given moment.

Setting a new goal of having a work-life blend wasn't an overnight remedy, but in time, taking it allowed me to release some of the guilt and worry I'd been carrying. By accepting that work-life balance is a myth, I no longer felt like a failure when I spent a long day at my desk or during weeks when I had to phone it in at work because my personal life required more attention. Being able to step back from that shame-and-blame cycle felt so freeing, and ironically, it helped me find the peace that I'd been craving.

Why I Hate the Phrase *Work-Life Balance*

I know I'm not the only person who has allowed the pursuit of a work-life balance to create extra stress, because it's something that comes up a lot with my coaching clients. Just like me, they buy into the idea that to be successful, we need to achieve that perfect balance. They, too, believe that the best way to manage the pressures of having it all is by figuring out a fail-safe routine. They, too, get sucked into all the tips and hacks that are regurgitated in the media: Don't check your emails on the weekend! Block out a lunch hour in your diary! Communicate your boundaries with your boss! But those tips, just like the phrase *work-life balance*, are incredibly reductive, ignoring the vast complexities and nuances that we all face.

The phrase *work-life balance* implies that we are all trying to balance just two things: work and life. Yet we all know that each of those areas can contain a vast array of priorities and demands. Work is a catchall for projects, meetings, self-development, training, and so much more. Don't even get me started on life, which encompasses everything from our homes to our health, our families to our hobbies, and all that lies in between.

And the word *balance* implies that we should be dedicating equal amounts of time and energy to each, something that isn't possible or perhaps even desirable to most women. I know from working with my clients that some of them aspire to work as little as possible so they have more time to dedicate to their kids or to their hobbies, while others take so much joy from their work that they're happy to give it more focus than they do other areas of their life. And importantly, the weight we give each might change throughout our lives, reflecting our experiences and circumstances.For example, right now, I'm in a season of life when I'm the mum of a toddler. That means that my "life" category is pretty full, with playdates, teething, and the practical load of caregiving taking up the vast majority of my time. However, when my daughter starts school in a few years' time, I know that the pendulum will start to swing back in the other direction, and work might take up more of my focus.

The language we use doesn't reflect the realities I see in mine, my friends', or my clients' lives. How do you achieve perfect balance when you're caring for a child with additional needs while also trying to make ends meet financially? How do you achieve perfect balance when you're managing a health condition while also trying to show up for your career? How do you achieve perfect balance when you're experiencing a complicated fertility journey or navigating redundancy?

We all face different, complex challenges. It's essential to recognise this, as so often we spend time and energy trying to pursue what might be impossible to achieve or that doesn't even align with our desires. We set ourselves up to fail, and when we do, rather than pausing to interrogate why, we internalise it as a personal failure, just like I did in those early days of running my business. It's time to stop striving for things that don't serve us and instead channel that energy into getting stuff done and embracing the blend. Perhaps you'll find that you might just end up feeling more balanced as a result.

✹ *Try* This ✹

Think about your tasks and responsibilities at work, your domestic duties, your caring responsibilities, your hobbies, your relationships, the ways you care for your health, the actions you take towards reaching personal goals, and anything else that might come to mind. Don't forget to think about the mental load too, considering things like managing your children's social commitments, maintaining familial ties, and checking in on friends. Write a list of everything you are trying to balance.

Then, reflect on your list. How does it feel to see it all written down?

There are two reasons why I invite you to complete this task. Firstly, it will help you start to identify what's important to include in your current blend. But perhaps most importantly, I hope that seeing everything you're trying to balance written down will help you practise greater self-compassion. Life is hard, and there's a lot to juggle. We're snowed under with visible and invisible labour, and the expectations placed on us are vast. Don't let those reductive balance hacks make you forget that.

Embracing the Blend

Five years into running my own business, I thought I was doing a perfect job of embracing a work-life blend. And then I became a mum. Suddenly, I'd thrown a new big priority into the mix, and I realised that the work-life blend I'd adopted for the last few years needed to change. I'll be honest, despite the fact that everyone had warned me how time-consuming children are while I was pregnant, I wasn't quite prepared for just how impacted my blend would be. I've seen the same thing happen with my coaching clients too. Take Rachel, for example. Her blend had always been very heavily skewed towards her work, and that had felt great to her. She loved the career she was building, and given that many of her colleagues had also become good friends, it made sense for her to spend lots of time socialising with them outside work too. But then some unexpected health challenges meant that Rachel had to make some big changes, dropping down to part-time hours to give her the space to navigate hospital appointments and recovery time. Work occupied less of her blend, so Rachel had to figure out what she wanted to fill that time with, redefining what success looked like in this chapter of life. She rediscovered her love of reading, something that had provided her with lots of joy as a child, and also started spending more time outdoors. Once Rachel returned to work full time, she found herself tweaking that blend once again, making sure to protect her new hobbies and her health while also giving more attention to the career she loved.

Our work-life blend will likely go through hundreds of iterations throughout our lives as we navigate changing priorities, curveballs, and identify shifts. Every season will bring its own blend, and all that matters is that we make sure we are intentional in deciding what it is rather than striving for some arbitrary sense of balance. And if you're wondering how you go about figuring out your work-life blend and what is most important to you in this season of life, I've got a process that might help you.

Four Steps to Building Your Blend

There are four key steps involved in building your blend. I've been using this process with my coaching clients and in corporate training sessions for years now. It's designed to help you figure out what you want to feature most prominently in your blend and then find ways to reduce the time and energy you need to spend on everything else.

Let me walk you through it step by step.

Build Your Blend Step 1: *Prioritise*

The first step is to identify what your priorities are. Take a moment to revisit the list of everything you are trying to balance that you made earlier and reflect on what is most important to you in this season of life, identifying two or three areas where you want to give it your best. Remember: you do not have to give your best to everything. In fact, it is impossible to do so. Get comfortable with focusing on the things that are most important to you and accepting that you can do an okay job at everything else.

I also want to remind you that you get to be one of your priorities. So often as women we can feel guilty for prioritising our own needs and carving out precious time for self-care, but it's essential that we do. As the saying goes, you can't pour from an empty cup, and success isn't success if it requires you to run yourself into the ground in order to achieve it.

A good way to start identifying your priorities is to think about how you want to feel now and in the coming months and work backwards from your answer. For example, if you want to feel accomplished, completing a big work project might be one of your priorities, or if you want to feel joyful, perhaps connecting with loved ones or practising gratitude will take up a spot on your list.

A few things to remember as you identify your priorities:

- There will be more than two or three things that you care about, but it's important to prioritise and choose the things that you most care about getting right.
- Your priorities can change over time. You don't need to decide what your biggest priorities are for the rest of your life. We are simply focusing on the season you are in right now, not looking more than three months in advance. For example, when I'm writing a book, it's one of my biggest priorities. But when I've finished a draft, my blend will change, and working on my fitness or giving more time to my hobbies might take its place.
- Try to let go of comparison as you identify your priorities and instead tune into what feels most true to you. You'll never feel like your blend is working for you if you're busy striving for someone else's goals. Stay connected to your own definition of success instead.

- You're allowed to choose things like joy and rest as your priorities—it doesn't all have to be about completing projects or achieving goals. Your well-being and happiness are just as (if not more!) important as any other outcome.

Build Your Blend Step 2: *Streamline*

The next three steps in figuring out your blend are all about exploring the changes you can make to free up more time and energy for the priorities you've identified, and you're going to start by looking at where you can streamline things. The idea with this step is to think about where you can take the mental and physical energies required to get the things on your to-do list done and redirect them towards your priorities.

Start by looking at your list of things you're trying to balance and consider if there's anything that would make your commitments easier to achieve. There might be some obvious things you can do. For example, you might do some batch cooking so that preparing meals is easier or you might automate your bill payments. But think outside the box too, and see if you can come up with any other ideas to reduce your energy output.

For example, when discussing this step with my client Ali, she spoke about how she spent a lot of mental energy on deciding when she would work out and what type of exercise she'd do. She packed her gym kit to take to work with her each day and would spend the whole day debating whether she'd go to the gym after work. She'd start by telling herself she absolutely would go, but as the day wore on and her stress levels increased, she'd find herself questioning that decision and wondering if it would be better for her to go straight home and relax. Often, this mental dance that she was performing throughout the day would require more energy than the actual workout itself! Once she realised this, Ali decided to start working out in the mornings so that she could get it over and done with and remove the decision-making process that was taking up so much energy each day.

Some things that might help with the streamlining step:

- Consider where you are spending a lot of energy but not getting much joy back—this is often a good place to focus on streamlining. Remember that you are allowed to use joy as one of your metrics of success!
- Consider what might be getting in the way of the type of rest you are

craving. For example, if you are craving a mental recharge, you might like to simply read news headlines instead of committing to the full article, freeing up more time for more rejuvenating activities.

- Ask your friends or loved ones how they make their to-do lists easier to deal with. Sometimes there are simple tricks right in front of us that we miss in the busyness of life.
- The actual act of streamlining can be boring and arduous (for example, creating a meal plan or setting up your bank account online). To cultivate the motivation required to take action, consider how you'll use the time you save. What joyful or restful experiences can you better fit into your life as a result of streamlining?

Build Your Blend Step 3: *Share*

The third step is to consider where you can share the load. Now, I want to preempt this step by warning you that this is where I see my clients experience the most resistance, particularly if they identify as people pleasers or pride themselves on being able to do it all themselves, as many women do. But I actually think Step Three is the most vital step for women in particular, as we so often take on more of the mental, emotional, and practical loads than our male counterparts, sometimes without even realising it.

For example, recently I delivered a workshop on using this process to an organisation, and one team member shared that she realised she had been taking on the full responsibility of making Christmas magical for her kids. She was the one who shopped for gifts, booked tickets to go to see Santa, organised festive playdates, bought the advent calendars, and, of course, made sure the day itself ran smoothly. While she loved being the magic maker, it also felt overwhelming to add so much to her to-do list during what was also a busy work period. She realised that her partner had never asked her to take full responsibility and in fact had tried to help numerous times, but she had been reluctant to relinquish control.

You might have had a similar experience. Perhaps you add more to your plate at work because you think that will make you look more competent, or perhaps you take on more of the domestic duties because you worry that your housemates or family members won't meet your high standards. Perhaps you feel guilty about how thinly stretched you are and add more to your to-do list to overcompensate—for example, trying to squeeze in many activities with your children on the weekend because you feel bad about not being as present during the workweek. It can sometimes even feel like keeping everything on your to-do list is more productive, especially if it would take time for you to brief or train someone else to support you. But when we are unwilling to share the load, we have less time for the things that help us achieve our visions of success.

A few things to consider as you explore where you could share the load:

- Asking someone for help doesn't mean you are placing a burden on them. Think about how great it feels when someone trusts you enough to seek your help. If you never ask, you are denying your loved ones that feeling.
- It might also be good to consider where asking someone for help might give them a sense of purpose—for example, your retired neighbour might feel great about being asked to help mow your lawn, as it gives them a focus for their day and makes them feel needed.
- Be really honest about what help you might be leaving on the table. I often hear people say that they don't have support when actually there are other things getting in the way of them accessing that support, such as pride, worry, or guilt.
- Sometimes, sharing the load might involve a financial transaction. For example, you might decide to pay someone to wash your car for you rather than washing it yourself if it gives you more time to spend on your priorities.

Build Your Blend Step 4: *Release (or Pause)*

The final step in streamlining is to consider what you can remove from your list completely—either forever or for this season of life. This is another step that can create some fear or resistance. When I ask people to consider what they can let go of, I'm often met with a response of "Nothing. It's all important, and it all needs to get done." But usually there is at least something we're spending time on that we can release, and if not, then we can certainly choose what to press pause on to help us navigate the season we're in.

Let me share with you some examples. My client Stacey was one of those people who believes that there is nothing they can let go of. However, as we dove a little deeper into where her time was going, she realised she was spending much more time scrolling on social media than she had first thought. As she worked in marketing, she couldn't delete the apps completely (and she didn't want to, as she enjoyed consuming content that inspired her), but instead she set some limits around how much time she could spend on social media each day so that she could free up more time for her priorities. I worked with another client, Emily, during the pandemic. We had started 2020 by mapping out her goals for the year, one of which was to complete a half-marathon. However, when the first lockdown rolled around, she quickly found herself with an increased workload and a new responsibility of homeschooling her children. Finding the time to get out for her training runs was becoming increasingly more challenging, and the guilt of missing them was hanging over her. Using this four-step process, and identifying what her priorities were in that season of life, gave Emily the permission to hit pause on her goal of running a half-marathon, freeing up mental and physical energy for the other stuff she cared about. (She returned to her original goal later in the year when her work-life blend shifted and she absolutely smashed her first half-marathon!)

And here's an example from my own life. When my daughter was born, I was gifted a few beautiful baby journals, the type you fill in each month and use to keep track of key milestones. Life was so busy that I never got around to filling in the journal and would quickly forget the dates or remarks I was supposed to be keeping track of. The guilt of not keeping these records for my daughter felt huge, especially when I compared myself to other mums who appeared to be able to do it with no stress, but in time, I accepted that I cared more about being present for her in the moment than I did about preserving all our memories perfectly. I donated the journals and instead found my own way of tracking our memories, releasing the idea of perfection as I did.

Here are some things to keep in mind as you think about what you want to release or press pause on:

- Is there anything on your list that you're doing because you think you should be doing it? I often say to my clients that the word *should* is a joy killer. If you're doing something out of a sense of obligation rather than because it's meaningful to you in some way, you would probably be happier and more productive if you let go of that thing.
- Taking a pause might be useful if there's anything you'd like to experiment with letting go of, as it can feel less like you're making a big commitment or setting yourself up to fail. Just make sure to set a date and time to check in and review how the pause has worked for you.

Now that we've walked through the four steps to building your blend, jot down your thoughts about the actions you can take to address each step of the process.

Prioritise:	Streamline:

Share:	Release:

A Note on Setting Boundaries

So far in this chapter, we've reflected on how we can better manage the things we have on our plates. But if we're going to be able to embrace the work-life blend in a way that allows us to honour our priorities and achieve our own unique definitions of success, we also need to talk about a topic that can make many of us feel uncomfortable: setting boundaries.

Setting boundaries can feel intimidating and perhaps even unsafe if you've never had healthy boundaries modelled to you, but they are an essential part of living a joyful and productive life. Setting—and honouring—our boundaries helps decrease stress, improve our emotional health, and protect ourselves from burnout. And boundaries can help improve our relationships, something that might seem counterintuitive to a people pleaser but makes sense when you pause to think about it. If we are honouring our own time, energy, and priorities, then when we show up for others, we're more likely to be patient, kind, and present as opposed to stressed and resentful. In fact, Brené Brown (2021) argues that in her research she's found that boundaries are a prerequisite for empathy and compassion.

In my experience of being in the workplace and supporting my coaching clients, it appears that women find it harder to set boundaries than men, something that seems to be backed up by the research. From a young age we socialise our girls to prioritise the needs of others—you only have to walk down the toy aisle in any store to see the girls' section jam-packed with dolls and nurture role-play toys, while the boys get all the vehicles and dinosaurs. And women also face what Sheryl Sandberg refers to in her book, *Lean In: Women, Work, and the Will to Lead* (2013), as the *likeability penalty*—put simply, we expect men to be assertive, so it feels natural when they are, whereas we expect women to be kind and community focused, and so when we assert our boundaries, we run the risk of being liked less. And as we discussed earlier, likeability impacts our chances of success in the workplace.

So yes, there are some very real blocks to us setting boundaries, but they are an essential part of building a joyfully productive life and caring for our own well-being. If you have no idea where to get started with identifying and implementing boundaries that will support your goals, I've got a handy little process that might help you. I use this at least once a week in my own life, and I hope it might be helpful for you too.

Setting Boundaries Step 1: *Identify the Need*

This is where you can revisit the priorities you outlined earlier, or your wider definition of success. What do you want or need more time and energy for?

For example, right now, I'm craving more time to myself. Having a young daughter and a thriving business means I don't often get a lot of time to rest and recharge, but it's a big priority for me in this season of life.

Setting Boundaries Step 2: *Identify the Boundary*

Consider what gets in the way of you focusing on your priorities. What can help you avoid the obstacles to sticking with your priorities and stop people from encroaching on your time?

Following on from my earlier example, the boundary I need to set is to create a clearer separation between work and life. This looks like not checking my emails after a certain time of day and also communicating to clients how long they can expect to wait for a reply from me so that I can fully switch off when I'm not at my desk.

Setting Boundaries Step 3: *Identify the Benefits*

Take some time to reflect on what lies on the other side of the boundary for you. What will improve if you protect your time and energy? It can also help to consider what might get better for the things and people you care about—for example, how might your employer or family benefit from you setting the boundary?

I know that if I can create a clear boundary between work and life, I will be a much more present mother and will find myself wanting to check my phone less. It also means that my clients will receive better service from me, as their response will be more well thought-out rather than dashed off as I also try to make my daughter's lunch. Finally, I know that I will feel calmer and find it easier to be present for the things that bring me joy.

Setting Boundaries Step 4: *Activate and Reflect*

Finally, set the boundary and take action to maintain it. Remember, we're focusing on the smallest step here rather than jumping headfirst into any bold changes. Once you've set the boundary and are working to keep it solid, take some time to reflect on what you've learnt. Is the boundary the right one? Does it need to be amended in any way or replaced with a different one?

Once I've set my work boundary, I will review it in a couple of weeks' time to see how it's going. I might notice that I want to change the times involved in the boundary, or perhaps I'll recognise that I need to communicate more clearly with others. Regardless, I know that having this time to reflect is essential if I want to uphold the boundary.

Remember: there is no perfect boundary, and the boundaries you need will likely change depending on the season you're in and the work-life blend you're trying to achieve.

One of the things I've seen my clients struggle with is communicating their boundaries to other people. This can feel particularly challenging if you've struggled to assert your own needs in the past. I've developed a formula of sorts that can help you put your needs and boundaries into words. Here's how it goes:

I feel . . . when . . . because . . . therefore, I need . . .

Here are some examples:

- "I feel overwhelmed when I have too many social plans because I'm also having a busy time at work. Therefore, I need to protect my weekends for the next few months while I deliver this project, meaning I won't be able to make it to your birthday party. Thanks again for the invite and have a great time!"
- "I feel stressed when I overcommit myself financially, as I'm trying to save to move house. Therefore, I need to skip the beach trip this year, but I'll look forward to joining again next year. "
- "I feel confused when I take on too many new projects at work because I struggle to know where to focus my time and energy. Therefore, I need you to help clarify the priorities and look at what extra resources we have to help us deliver our objectives as a team."

When you communicate your needs clearly, it's difficult for anyone to argue with your boundaries, and it will help you uphold them more effectively.

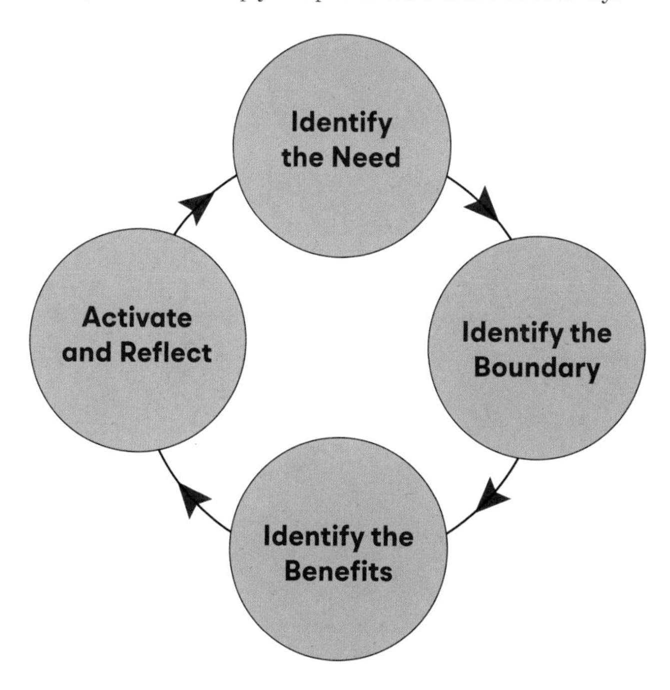

Finding Your Flow

Before we explore some tips on how to embrace a work-life blend depending on your productivity archetype, there's one last topic I want to explore, and that's the concept of flow. Colloquially referred to as being *in the zone*, flow refers to a state in which a person is fully immersed in a feeling of energised focus and enjoyment. It's an incredibly important ingredient for joyful productivity. Research shows that entering a flow state increases our focus, improves the volume and quality of our output, creates a sense of enjoyment, and improves our well-being.

These benefits are important to note as we consider the idea of embracing the blend, because they demonstrate the importance of slowing down and focusing on one thing at a time, as opposed to trying to balance everything harmoniously and flitting from one task to the next. This is particularly important given that women may feel more pressure to multitask in order to manage all the competing demands on their time. Additionally, I believe that what many of us are seeking when we set ourselves the goal of balance—a sense of focus, clarity, and harmony—can be achieved by experiencing a flow state.

According to Mihaly Csikszentmihalyi (1989), the positive psychologist who led the bulk of the research into the concept of flow, there are a few key requirements that need to be met to enter a flow state:

- You must care about the task at hand and be motivated to complete it. In other words, it must be a priority or goal that feels authentic to you, as opposed to something you feel like you should complete.
- There must be a balance between challenge and skill. If the task is too easy, you'll be bored and distracted; if the task is too hard, you'll be more likely to procrastinate or give up. You need to be able to use your strengths but also be able to stretch your comfort zone a little.
- You must be motivated by the process, not just the outcome. Solely focusing on achievement isn't as effective as enjoying the experience of getting there.
- You must find a sense of enjoyment in the task, even if you don't enjoy every element.

The process of writing this book allowed me to enter a flow state. I care deeply about the content of this book and presenting it to the world in an accessible way. Writing this book is something I wanted to do, not something that was on my to-do list because I felt like I should achieve that goal. I wrote my debut book a few years ago, and that allowed me to hone my skills, and I have vast experience dealing with the topics in this book. However, there is still plenty of challenge that comes with presenting research in an interesting way and constructing a compelling narrative. I'm motivated by the process of writing the book, as it allows me to think more deeply about topics that I perhaps wouldn't otherwise get an opportunity to spend so much time researching. So, while it can sometimes be challenging to find the time to sit and write, I really do enjoy writing. All these factors help me find flow, which in turn helps me be productive, find joy, and experience the other benefits listed earlier.

DO IT YOUR WAY

Think about a time when you've experienced being in a flow state. What was happening? What was your environment like? What can you learn from your experience?

Then take another look at your list of the things you're trying to balance and think about which items or activities might present an opportunity to enter a flow state.

Embracing the Blend Depending on Your Productivity Archetype

We've covered a lot in this chapter, but before we round it out, I want to share some tips and watch-outs for each productivity archetype when it comes to embracing the blend and finding your flow.

The Doer

If you identify as a doer, be careful not to let the quest for balance mean that you end up adding more to your plate. Let me share a little example from my own life here. In one of my previous roles, I had to spend a night or two a week in London so that I could be present in our head office. I'd spend three hours commuting ahead of a long day of client meetings and would often have to be back in the office before eight a.m. the following day, but rather than heading to my hotel to rest and recharge in the evening, I'd always try to squeeze in dinner with friends or a visit to an exhibition or show. I tried to convince myself that getting to see friends or squeezing in some culture meant I was achieving some sort of work-life blend, but in truth, I was simply stretching myself more than I had capacity for. My priority in this season was work, and I needed to be able to recharge in order to do my best work. It would have been much more sustainable for me to take the blend approach we discussed in this chapter, dedicating my time and focus to my work while I was in London and then leaning more heavily into my personal life during the rest of the week, or booking a trip to return to London in my own time during a season when connection or leisure was a bigger priority for me.

The Perfectionist

If you identify as a perfectionist, your biggest hurdle will likely be accepting the reality that you'll never find a perfect work-life blend. This will be especially true if you've spent the majority of your life to date striving to find that perfect blend, always believing that you were just touching distance away, or if you have been raised to place particular importance on the idea of having it all, believing that you could simultaneously be a "perfect" mother, wife, colleague, and friend. But trust me when I say that by aiming for a blend that works for you, not only will you be more productive, but you'll also experience more joy and fulfilment. This was the case for my client Holly, a classic perfectionist who found it challenging to step away from her colour-coded schedules and jam-packed days. However, she committed to the Build Your Blend process I shared in this chapter, and it helped her focus more on the things that were important to her—namely, delivering her core objectives at work while also travelling as much as possible. She began taking the time to be fully present on her trips rather than trying to squeeze in emails or personal development like she had done previously. Consequently, she returned to work feeling rested and creative, which in turn helped her be more productive.

The Dreamer

Of the dreamers I've worked with, the biggest challenge I see them face is shiny magpie syndrome, otherwise known as being distracted by new goals and priorities before they've had the chance to fully honour their previous ones. If this rings true for you, the most important action for you to take is to get crystal clear on your priorities for whatever season you're in and to commit to them. I've found that something that works for the dreamers I coach is setting a shorter time frame and identifying priorities for that period. For example, taking the next month and being specific about the two to three things you want to give the most time and energy to. Then keep a list of anything else that comes to mind while you're working on those priorities, or any new ideas you may have. That way, you can trust that you won't forget the ideas, and you'll have a place to start from when it comes to reevaluating your blend.

The Procrastinator

Finally, if you identify as a procrastinator, you might find you resist sharing the load or streamlining tasks, as not doing so gives you a pool of activities to dive into whenever you want to procrastinate your priorities. Dipping into those tasks can feel a lot less overwhelming than tackling the goals that will create a big change for you, and so it's totally natural to want to keep them close at hand, but it will be challenging to create the change you want to achieve if you do. It can be helpful to create some accountability around completing those steps by working through them with someone else. This is what my client Amy did—she completed the Build Your Blend process with her sister, who was then able to act as an accountability buddy and check in to see how she was getting on. The fact that her sister also knew Amy's biggest priorities meant that Amy had someone to remind her of what was most important to her and check in on her progress.

I often say that one of the biggest privileges of being a coach is that I get to peek behind the scenes of other people's lives. I have had the honour of supporting a vast array of women, who have achieved all sorts of incredible things, and I want to tell you this: I have never come across anyone with a perfect balance or routine. The most successful, joyful, and healthy women I know will readily admit that their lives are messy and often chaotic, with priorities changing from week to week or month to month. We might crave routine, balance, and predictability, but the truth is that for the majority of us, life rarely provides us with the conditions that make that possible. Workloads vary, our kids get sick, we experience the seasonal and cyclical changes explored in previous chapters, and so much more.

We need to stop holding ourselves to an impossible standard, and we need to let go of the guilt and shame that might arise when our lives look and feel a little messier than we think they should. When we embrace a more fluid and forgiving approach to managing our time and energy, not only do we give ourselves a better chance of achieving our own definitions of success in whatever season of life we're in, but we also honour our humanity. We're not robots—we need to stop expecting ourselves to act like them. Instead, trust that your intuition will guide you to find a blend that works for you. You might just find that life feels more harmonious and joyful as a result.

LET'S RECAP

- **Work-life balance is a reductive ambition, one that doesn't account for the many challenges and commitments we have and our fluctuating priorities.**
- **Learning to embrace a work-life blend can help us not only to live more harmoniously but also reduce guilt and worry, both of which can be mentally and physically draining.**
- **The four-step process of prioritise, streamline, share, and release (or pause) can help us identify where to focus our time and energy in any given season of life.**
- **Setting boundaries and finding flow are also useful tools in embracing the blend.**

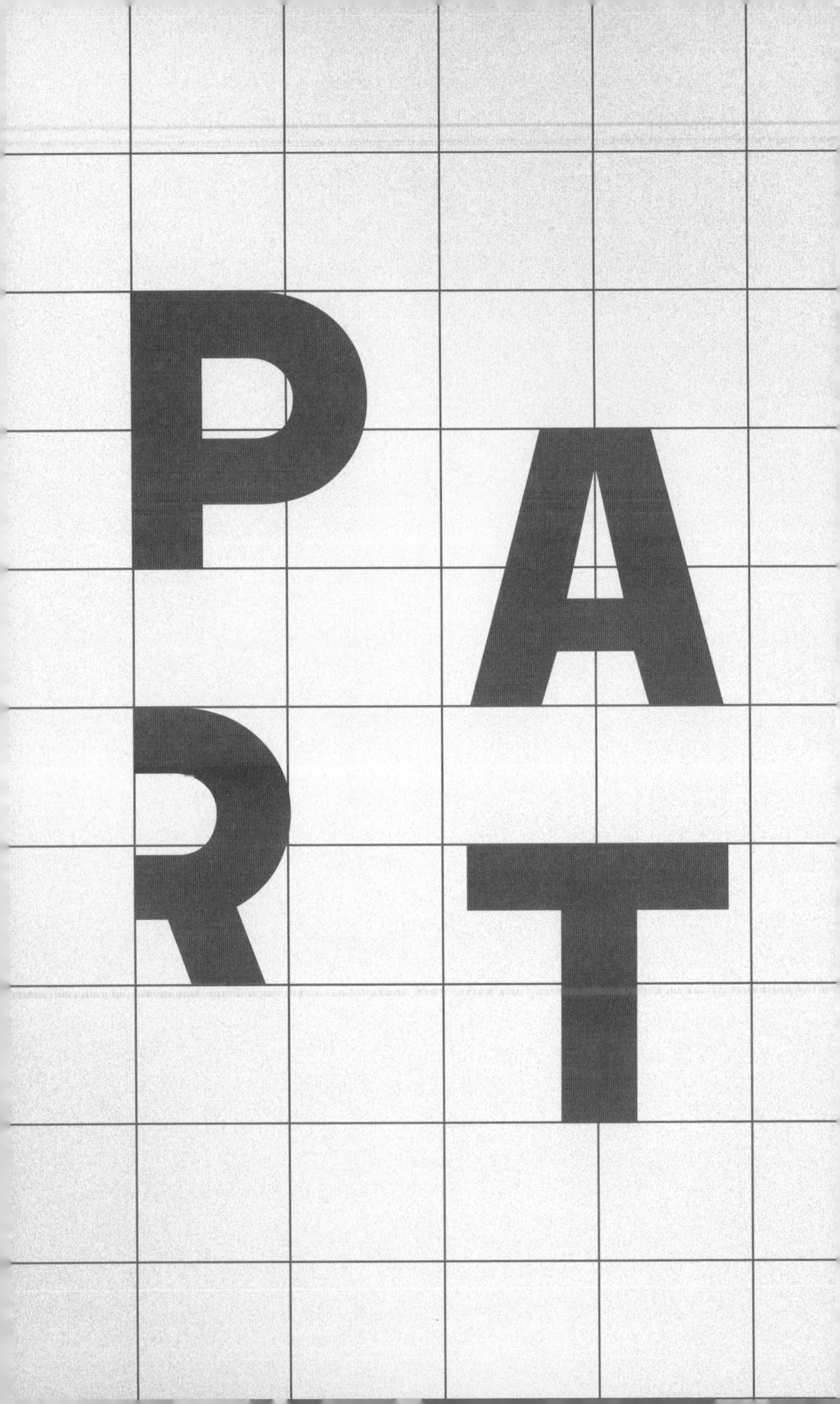
PART

3

CHAPTER 9:

DISCOVER THE JOY METHOD

When I first pitched this book to my publisher, my top priority was to ensure it would be practical and actionable. I have spent a long time now watching women chase other people's versions of success, making themselves miserable or unwell in the process. I have spent too long watching the patriarchal, capitalistic structures we exist within trap us in a toxic cycle of productivity. I have listened to too many women as they have told me that they are the problem, that if they were just more productive or disciplined or focused, they could finally be happy.

I hope you have realised by now that we are not the problem, and I hope you feel excited about approaching productivity and success in a new way. But I also imagine that you are very tired. The very fact that you've picked up this book suggests that you're likely a woman with a lot on her plate, feeling busy and overwhelmed. You likely feel pulled in many directions, trying to satisfy competing demands while also managing your own well-being and desires in the process. I know from experience that when you're in that state, it can be challenging to figure out where to start and how to put new information into practice.

I've often found myself reading a book, thinking, "Wow, that's going to change my life," only to struggle to remember the key takeaways a few weeks later. I don't want you to have that experience with this book. As you've probably gathered from what you've read so far, I'm deeply passionate about transforming the ways we view and experience productivity. I'm committed to helping you make lasting changes that will lead to more joy and authentic success in your life.

That's why I'm dedicating the rest of this book to guiding you through the process of creating a personalised action plan—one that will not only enhance your productivity but also ensure that the journey feels joyful, purposeful, and sustainable to you. We will make sure that your plan is tailored to your unique experiences, personality, and circumstances because, as we've discussed, a one-size-fits-all approach rarely leads to the desired outcomes. We'll also explore how you can adapt your plan to accommodate the different seasons and energetic cycles you'll encounter throughout your life.

The approach we'll be using is an approach I call the Joy Method. It's a framework I've applied consistently in my own life, helping me achieve goals both big and small—from completing my master's programme and writing my first book to building a consistent exercise habit and prioritising more time for my hobbies. I've also used this method with hundreds of clients, supporting them in designing the lives they truly want to live. Because that's what joyful productivity is all about: not just racking up achievements for the sake of it but making meaningful changes that allow you to give more focus to what matters most.

I call it the Joy Method because it emphasises the importance of experiencing joy throughout the process of making changes and achieving goals. Every step of this method has joy at its heart, because, as you've likely come to realise by now, when we keep joy as our North Star, everything we care about becomes more manageable and fulfilling. As women, we sometimes need that reminder to prioritise our own joy rather than always put everyone else's needs first. It also weaves together the topics and tools we've discussed in earlier chapters, from embracing your intuition and unique strengths to honouring your energetic cycles and finding flow.

In this chapter, I'll walk you through each step of the Joy Method in detail, referencing some of the tools we've discussed so far and demonstrating how they fit into the overall framework. Then in the next chapter, I'll provide guidance on how to apply the Joy Method to your own life, with a focus on tailoring it to your specific productivity archetype.

Let's get started.

Introducing the Joy Method

The Joy Method is composed of four steps:

1. Defining success for you
2. Identifying your strengths and strategies
3. Taking joyful action
4. Reflecting and learning

Each of these steps has joy at its core. Working through them in turn will help you not only get more done but make sure you're pouring your efforts into getting the right things done—the things that will make your life feel more joyful.

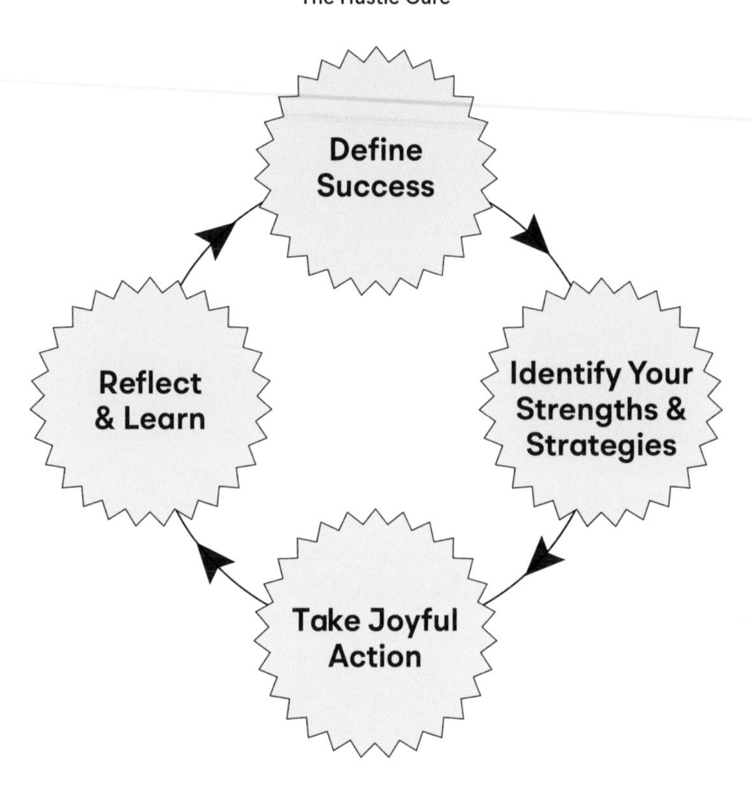

You'll notice from the diagram above that the steps repeat, forever feeding into one another. That's because the Joy Method is an iterative process: every time you work through the four steps, you'll learn something new that may reshape your vision of success or help you develop new strengths or strategies that can inspire new actions. Plus, life changes, and so do we as individuals.

A key part to living a joyful life is recognising this and staying flexible as we navigate different seasons, and this method acknowledges that. If we want to experience joy, we can't be putting all our energy into achieving some sort of happily ever after. Instead, we should strive to prioritise the most important things to us in the season we are in—and find joy as we address what is at the top of our list.

You can use the Joy Method to achieve anything you want to achieve and be more joyful and productive in the pursuit, whether you are working towards a big life goal, such as changing your career or buying your first home, or something smaller—for example, starting a new hobby or trying to improve your fitness. You will find some illustrative examples from my own experience and that of my clients woven through the steps and integrated into the end of the chapter.

It's essential that you give each step the attention it needs. You will likely prefer some steps over others depending on your productivity archetype, but in the next chapter, I'll share plenty of tips to help you put the method into action so that it impacts your life as much as possible.

For now, let's dive into each step in more detail.

Step 1: Define Success for You

The first step in the Joy Method is to define what success looks like for you. This might not come as a big surprise given that we spent the first few chapters exploring the need to let go of other people's markers of success and build an authentic vision for ourselves. However, I know that sticking to a new, personalised definition of success isn't always that easy to do, particularly if you have been conditioned since childhood to meet the expectations of others, as many of us are.

And I know that because I've had a lot of experience setting goals for myself without ever considering what my own definition of success was. I was particularly vulnerable to taking this approach when it came to my career. Whenever I felt stuck in a rut or frustrated at work (which was more often than I ever liked to admit), I'd try to re-energise myself by diving headfirst into some new goals. Sometimes, the goal would be to get a new job or a promotion. Other times, it would be about developing a new skill or trying to build my reputation within the organisation. What I never did was stop to ask myself why I was setting these goals or what I was hoping to gain by ticking them off the list.

However, that lack of reflection didn't get in the way of me achieving my goals. By the time I was twenty-eight, I had some of the biggest global brands on my CV and was heading up a team of eighty people. I'd travelled to incredible places as part of my job and achieved a benefits package that teenage me would never have dreamt was possible, and my job title always earned a nod of respect. I'd ticked off some impressive career achievements, yet I didn't feel successful. Instead, what I felt was a creeping sense of claustrophobia. The higher I climbed, the more that was required of me and the less sure I was that this was what I wanted. That feeling of uncertainty, combined with multiple bouts of burnout, left me in a tricky place. My anxiety was at an all-time high, my confidence was on the floor, and I lacked purpose and meaning.

This is what happens when we don't define success on our own terms, when we instead pursue the version of success that has been presented to us by society or the people around us. In trying to keep up with others or prove ourselves in some way, we run ourselves into the ground and sacrifice our own happiness and health in the process. Because I had never taken the time to check in and get clear on what I actually wanted, it didn't matter how much I achieved or how productive I managed to be: it never felt joyful or sufficient. You might have had a similar experience. When we're in that place of ploughing through to achieve a goal that we are not even certain we want to reach, there's no productivity hack or time management trick that will help us. Instead, what we need is clarity about our own definition of success.

It was only when I took the time to figure out how I wanted to define success in my career that I was able to start focusing my energy and effort on the actions that would make a real difference. My productivity skyrocketed as a result. When you know why you want to achieve something, and when you can trust that doing so will add more joy to your life, you don't need to rely on willpower or discipline to see you through. And that's what I love about the Joy Method: it's not about being less ambitious if that doesn't feel right to you. (I have achieved more in my career since getting clear on my definition of success than I ever could have before.) Instead, it's about focusing your ambition on the right things. Understanding that was a game changer for me, and I know it will be for you too.

So, we start the Joy Method by defining what you want to achieve or change and getting clear on what success will look like. And as you might have guessed from what you've already read, we're going to put a whole lot of emphasis on making sure that you are focused on your version of success, not the one that you've been taught to strive for or that will help you keep up with your peers. Because it's only when we're working towards our own authentic goals that our efforts will make us feel more joyful and fulfilled.

A good place to start to figure out where to focus your energy is to revisit the exercises in Chapter Three. (If you haven't had a chance to complete them yet, now is the time!) Start with the Try This exercise on page 38. Which area of your life felt least successful when you were using joy as your measure of success? Spend some time exploring the changes or goals that could help you up the score. The other exercise worth revisiting is the Best Possible Self exercise on page 46. Your answers to that exercise should contain some pretty strong clues about the changes or goals that you could work towards to start making your life feel more joyful and authentically successful.

Once you have identified a goal or change that you'd like to use the Joy Method to help you achieve, there are two other important things to consider. The first is getting clear on why you want to achieve this specific goal, and the second is getting clear on how you'll know you're successful.

It's vital to be clear on your reasons for your goal for two reasons. Firstly, it will help you assess whether this is something that truly feels important and authentic to you. If you can explain with gusto why you want to make the changes you've outlined or achieve a certain goal, and if you can clearly see how it will move you closer to your definition of success, you'll know for sure that it's something you truly want and not just something you're pursuing because you feel like you should or because you want to keep up with or impress someone else.

For example, after working through some of the exercises I've shared with you in this book, my client Lucy decided that success for her looked like relocating to the seaside. She loves being by the sea, and she always felt more joyful and grounded when she was visiting her friend who lived in a coastal town, but she still had some doubts about whether this was the right move for her given that her career was based in London, where she'd been living for the past ten years. However, when I asked her to get clear on why she wanted to relocate, she spoke passionately about her desire to slow down, to be in nature, to spend more time doing the things that bring her joy, instead of letting her schedule be utterly consumed by work. Her answer to that question came so naturally and was so heartfelt that she was able to feel more confident that she'd landed on the right goal and the right definition of success for her.

The other reason why it's important to explore the why behind your goal is that it will help you build motivation to take action. We'll talk more about taking action in a later step, but if you're clear on the reasons why working towards your goal will benefit you, you'll find it much easier to stay inspired and committed during the process of making a change. Lucy certainly found this. There were many times when it felt like the act of uprooting her life and moving hours away from everything she'd known was simply too hard, but remembering that all her hard work would facilitate the slowing down she was craving gave her that extra bit of gusto when she most needed it.

The other important thing to do when you've outlined the goal or change you'd like to make is to get clear on how you'll know when you've been successful. You've probably heard that making our goals and objectives measurable is a key part of being able to achieve them, and this case is no different! If you don't have some markers of success that you can check in with along the way, it will be difficult to measure the progress that you're making and, worse still, you might miss that glorious moment of realising that you've achieved something you've long been striving for.

There's something about setting tangible measurements or markers that can make us revert back to those old productivity beliefs and convince ourselves that we need to set bold or impressive targets to make our efforts worthwhile. I want to remind you to keep joy as your focus here and to give yourself permission to set clear goals for yourself that will help you reach your version of success in an enjoyable way.

Let me give you an example from my own life. I mentioned earlier that I spent many years setting goals for my career that weren't rooted in my own version of success. In 2018, I changed that, and after doing lots of work exploring what was most important to me and what would bring me more joy, I decided to make a career change and retrain as a coach and psychologist. When it came to setting myself some measurable markers that I could use to know I'd achieved my version of success, my brain automatically went to classic career objectives, such as hitting a certain income goal or booking a certain number of clients. But when I challenged myself to really think about how I'd know I'd achieved my version of success, the answer was different: I'd know I'd been successful when I had the flexibility and freedom to wrap up work early and pick up my nephew from school. I'd know I'd been successful when I could look back on my week and know that my work had made a positive impact. Outlining those measures of success before embarking on that change meant that I could avoid getting distracted by goals or achievements that weren't my number one priority and that when I stood at the school gates waiting for my nephew, or when I closed my laptop on a Friday afternoon knowing that I'd been able to truly help my clients, I could celebrate that moment and enjoy the feeling of success.

It might be useful to write both your why and your markers of success down somewhere so that you can return to them when you need them.

Here are a few more points to note when you're defining your version of success:

- Consider your blend. What do you need to prioritise to achieve your goal, and what might you have to streamline, share, or let go of to create time and energy for those priorities?
- Be aware of how societal expectations and experiences creep in. Try to let go of what will make you a "good" girl, daughter, mother, or friend (or any other title) and instead tune into your own desires.

- If you're drawing a bit of a blank when it comes to setting a goal, think about how you want to feel and what actions or changes would help you cultivate that feeling. When I was planning my career change, I didn't always know the exact details of what I wanted my new career to hold, but I knew I wanted to feel more free and joyful in my work, and that gave me a good basis from which to explore some changes. Similarly, I worked with a client who wanted her life to feel adventurous. Starting from that feeling helped us explore some tangible goals, such as planning a solo trip or trying out a new creative class.
- Try to let go of what anybody else might think about your goal. Remember that your aim is to become clear about your definition of success and add more joy to your life, not anybody else's. The chances are that you've already tried striving for someone else's version of success and it hasn't made you as happy as you'd hoped—it's time to give trusting yourself a go instead.
- On that note, there is no right or wrong when it comes to defining success on your own terms. You might find that you want to scale back your goals and live a simpler life, or perhaps you'll find that you have huge ambitions that you want to strive towards. Neither is more worthy than the other. All that matters is that your definition feels authentic and purposeful to you. Let go of what anybody else might think. They don't have to live your life—you do.

Step 2: Identify Your Strengths & Strategies

Once you've identified the change or goal you'd like to achieve, the next step is to figure out the strengths and strategies you'll adopt to help you get there. And we're going to approach this challenge in a different way than you might have done in the past.

As we've already discussed in previous chapters, often when we set ourselves a goal or think about a change we want to make, our immediate next step is to seek external advice or guidance. We assume that someone else will have more expertise than us and that it will be more efficient and productive to extract that information from them and apply it to our own lives. But when we do that, we end up pouring energy into actions or strategies that either don't move us closer to our version of success or take too much effort to execute, making them unsustainable. Plus, when we are trying to implement someone else's plan or advice to help us achieve our goals, we are less likely to find joy in the process.

I spent most of my adult life using this approach to try to help me build a consistent exercise habit. I would come to the realisation that feeling fitter would help me enjoy life more, but rather than pausing to consider which of my resources and strengths I could use to build an exercise habit that supported my fitness goals, I would immediately turn to Google to see what someone else would recommend, or rely heavily on the advice of a personal trainer or gym instructor. I'd start the process feeling buoyed by having a detailed plan provided by an expert, but as time went on, I'd always encounter some sort of obstacle. Maybe it was that the plan required me to work out at a frequency or time of day that didn't support my energy cycle, or perhaps it didn't feel challenging enough to me, which would make it difficult for me to experience a sense of flow. Maybe the plan didn't add much joy to my life. Or perhaps the plan just didn't work for the current work-life blend I was working towards.

I didn't crack making exercise a consistent habit until I got clear on my own strengths and strategies and used them to help me craft a plan. Not only has approaching my goals and plans using this approach helped me have greater success, but it's also worked wonders for my confidence. No longer do I get caught in the shame-and-blame cycle—instead, I find I have a much greater success rate with my goals and get to experience lots of joy in the process too.

Here are a few tips to help you identify the strengths and strategies that will help you achieve your desired goal or change:

Create your energy profile

In Chapter Five, we explored the role of energy and considered our own unique energy cycles, and that topic is a great place to start when it comes to identifying your strategies. If you can ensure that your actions are planned in-line with your unique energy cycles, you'll give yourself a much greater chance of achieving what you've set out to achieve, and you'll be less likely to quit or burn out in the process.

Something I like to encourage my clients to do when they are setting off towards a new goal is to create an energy profile. This can act as a reminder to them of when they're likely to be at their best and what can support them when they're experiencing an energetic slump.

You can use the template below to create your own energy profile.

1. The time of day or night when I feel most energetic is . . .

2. This is how I feel at different points in my cycle:

3. This how I feel during the different seasons of the year:

Spring:

Summer:

Winter:

Fall:

4. The things most likely to drain my energy are . . .

5. The things that help me restore my energy are . . .

6. When I'm at my most energetic, I am prioritising . . .

7. Other things to note about my energy are . . .

Once you've completed your energy profile, consider how it might impact the way you go about achieving your goal. For example, I'm most energetic before lunchtime, so when I was working on my goal of creating a consistent exercise habit, I tried to plan my workouts for the morning. I also have pretty big energetic fluctuations throughout my monthly cycle, and I adapt the way I exercise to accommodate for that. For example, when I'm ovulating, I might choose a more energetic workout, such as a spin class or a jog, whereas when I'm menstruating, I'm more likely to stick to a walk or a gentle yoga class. Taking my energy into account when working on this goal has been a huge factor in making my exercise habit sustainable, and it's also helped me enjoy working out more.

Consult your intuition

The next thing that can help you identify the strategies that will work best for you is to consult your intuition. As we explored in Chapter Six, intuition is an incredibly powerful resource, and it's likely that using your intuition to help you identify actions and strategies is more useful and productive than turning to Google. Here are a few ways that you can do that:

- Notice the first ideas that come to your mind. Something I've noticed from working with my coaching clients is that often the first idea we have is usually pretty on the money, but we end up bypassing it or talking ourselves out of it because we tell ourselves we haven't thought it through enough. Those first ideas are worth listening to, even if they feel a bit random or unorthodox. For example, when I was first starting to work on my goal of improving my fitness, I had a desire to swim outdoors in the sea or a lake. At the time, I had the thought that it wasn't something I'd ever done before, and it felt a bit too "outdoorsy" for a homebody like me, so I dismissed it out of hand. A few months later, my mother-in-law invited me to join her for a swim in the bay near her house, and I adored it! It made me wish I'd listened to that first thought earlier.
- Listen to your body. Once you have a few different ideas in your mind, take a few moments to sit quietly and be still. Then think about each idea in turn, tuning into what is happening in your body as you do so. You might feel yourself tense up at the thought of doing something that goes against your intuition, whereas you might experience a sense of lightness or excitement when you consider an option that feels good to you. You can use this exercise whenever you're making a decision and need to break away from going over and over the pros and cons list in your head.

- Journal. Sit down with a notebook and a pen and write about your goal and how you might go about achieving it. There's something about putting pen to paper and using your hand that can loosen up the creative muscles and get your intuition flowing. Don't worry about how neat your handwriting is or even what you're writing—it's the process that is more important than the output.

Supercharge your strengths

As you learnt in Chapter Seven, using your strengths is a powerful way to both improve your productivity and increase the amount of joy you experience. When it comes to achieving a goal or making a change, considering how we can best put our strengths into action is one of the most useful tools we have, but it's often overlooked.

I believe the reason we so often overlook our strengths is because it can sometimes be difficult to see how we can best use them in the pursuit of different goals. For example, I worked with a client, Sarah, who had a goal of being more present when she was with her children. This was something she'd struggled with in the past, often feeling distracted or like her mind was still on work even when she'd left the office. When we were exploring strategies that might help Sarah achieve this goal, I encouraged her to consider her strengths, one of which is having a love of learning. This felt tricky to Sarah—she could see how this strength had helped her do well at school and progress in her career, but she didn't think it was as relevant to her role as a parent or particularly useful for the goal she had outlined. However, once we discussed it further, Sarah could see that her love of learning meant she had the skills to research mindfulness techniques that might help her, and she was also very comfortable with adopting a beginner's mindset, something that helped her be more compassionate with herself as she worked towards this goal. No matter what your strengths are, there is a way for you to put them to good use—you just might need to get a bit creative!

Take some time to revisit your list of strengths from Chapter Seven and think about how you can employ them as you work towards your goal. You'll find that you feel a lot more motivated and productive as a result.

Find your flow

We explored the power of entering a flow state in Chapter Eight, and finding your flow can be another useful tool to consider when it comes to making your goal game plan. The most important thing to remember is that to enter a flow state, you need to experience both an adequate sense of challenge and an element of enjoyment, so keep both of these factors in mind when thinking about how you could best achieve your goal. You might also like to clear any distractions that could get in the way.

Finding my flow was a really useful strategy for me when working on my exercise habit, and it helped me see where I'd gone wrong previously. I'd been either choosing workouts that didn't feel challenging and becoming bored easily or forcing myself to do things I didn't actually enjoy. (Let me tell you that mustering up the energy to do a HIIT class felt nigh on impossible to me!) Now my favourite way to exercise is using my Peloton Bike—it definitely feels challenging, but the range of fun music and personable instructors means I also find it really enjoyable. For someone else, biking outdoors in nature, or with a friend, might make a difference.

The key to this step is giving yourself permission to find your best approach instead of getting swept up in someone else's plan. Trust me when I say that you'll get more done when you do it your way.

Step 3: Take Joyful Action

So, we know what our desired goal or change is, we've gathered up the strengths and strategies that will best equip us, and now it's time for our next step: taking action. But we're not just talking about any old action—nope, only joyful action over here, please!

The reason why I draw that distinction is because when we hear the word action, it's very easy to fall into the old hustle mindset. Many of us have grown up believing the best way to achieve something is the quickest and seemingly most efficient way, and so when we start to think about taking action on our goals, it's natural for us to immediately jump to thinking about the fastest way of reaching our desired outcome.

However, in my experience, the quickest way is rarely the best way. Instead, as you start taking action, I want to invite you to consider the most joyful way of achieving your goal. Because when we take the joyful route, we feel good, and when we feel good, we're much more likely to keep showing up and taking more action, enabling us to achieve greater consistency and productivity over time.

My client Melissa certainly found this. We worked together after she had been made redundant in a workplace role that she'd been in for almost ten years. Melissa had initially been happy to accept a voluntary layoff, seeing it as an opportunity to shake up her career a little and try something new. However, after a few months of job seeking with no luck, she was starting to feel anxious about her next steps. Melissa had received some redundancy compensation, which meant that she had built herself a financial buffer, and she wanted to use the time between jobs to recharge and focus on her hobbies. However, the uncertainty meant she was spending all day every day at her desk, applying for multiple jobs a week and never letting herself relax. As a result, she was feeling tense and overwhelmed.

In one of our coaching sessions, I encouraged Melissa to think about how she would change her course of action if she were focusing on making it feel as joyful as possible. Melissa spoke about how she'd go to more networking meetups, as this appealed to her extroverted nature. She floated the idea of working on job applications from her favourite coffee shop, turning it into a little date with herself, and she said she'd love to take some time to take a course to develop new skills while she was between roles. Finally, she reminded herself that she wanted to keep focusing on her hobbies as she knew she might never have this sort of free time between roles again. By inviting the idea of joy to the process, Melissa was able to identify the actions that would energise her and allow her to continue seeking job opportunities without becoming burnt out or anxious.

I had the same experience with my goal of building my fitness. The reason why I also struggled to sustain an exercise habit in the past was because I bought into the idea that exercise is supposed to be difficult and punishing. As soon as I gave myself permission to have some fun, I released the resistance I was carrying and found it so much easier to prioritise the movement required to meet my goal. I never felt like going for a run, so I'd had to rely on discipline and willpower to get me out the door. Going to a yoga class with a friend or singing along during a *Hamilton*-themed Peloton class, on the other hand, requires no internal pep talks!

Here are some things that might help you identify and start taking joyful action:

- Look back at when you've enjoyed working towards a goal in the past. What was it about the way you worked towards that goal that made it enjoyable? This might inspire some ideas.
- Think about what you loved doing as a child. Children tend to be better at seeking joy than us adults, because they haven't yet learnt the "shoulds," so revisiting the ways we played as children might spark some ideas. For example, if you loved arts and crafts as a child, that might tell you to take a creative approach, or if you loved to be outside playing, that might remind you to adopt a spirit of adventure.
- Don't worry about taking perfect action. I see a lot of people get stuck in this step because they're waiting for the right time or they want to make sure they've identified the perfect action. Don't fall into that trap—doing something is always better than doing nothing!
- Don't have all your actions mapped out to begin—just identify the first joyful action, and then once you've completed that, figure out the next one. Baby steps!
- Remember that the value is in doing the thing. If you've grown up hearing things like *nothing worth having comes easy*, taking the joyful approach might feel unnatural or you might worry that it's not going to move you along, but joy is the difference between giving up and building a consistent habit.

Step 4: Reflect & Learn

The final step of the Joy Method is, in my opinion, the most important. Once we've defined success, identified our strengths and strategies, and taken joyful action, it's vital that we take some time to reflect and learn.

In my first book, *Choose Joy*, I included a quote from a man called John Dewey, and I'm going to include it again here. John Dewey was a philosopher, psychologist, and educational reformer, and he said: "We do not learn from experience . . . we learn from reflecting on experience." That for me sums up the importance of reflection. It's not just what we do that is important when it comes to joyful productivity, it's reflecting on what we've done and learning from our actions.

Here are some questions that might help you do that. You can use them as journaling prompts to answer in a notebook or as discussion points with friends. One of my clients, Alice, likes to record voice notes of her answers, as she finds she processes information more effectively when talking. It doesn't matter how you conduct your reflection, but what does matter is that you take the time to pause, review, and learn.

- What progress have I made in pursuit of my goal?
- As I move towards my goal, what is going well? What actions have I enjoyed? What strategies have helped move me forwards?
- What feels challenging? Why do I think that is? What ideas do I have about how to make those challenging aspects feel more joyful?
- What have I learnt about myself in this process?
- What action do I still need to take? What strengths and strategies do I have to help me?
- Does my definition of success feel true, or have I learnt or experienced anything that has changed it?
- Do I want to tweak my plan in any way?
- Is there anything else that is important for me to note at this stage in my pursuit of my definition of success?

Taking the time to reflect on these questions can provide a huge boost to your productivity for a number of reasons. Firstly, it will give you the opportunity to celebrate your progress and wins, which will improve your confidence and make you feel more motivated. Secondly, you'll have the opportunity to notice and troubleshoot any challenges before they become more overwhelming obstacles that could slow you down or knock you off course. You'll also find that regularly reflecting will allow you to tackle your goals in a more dynamic way and tweak your method and approach as you gather new information. But perhaps most importantly, taking the time to check in with yourself will supercharge your personal development. You'll learn new things about yourself and how you work best, you'll improve your relationship with your intuition, and you'll likely also develop a deeper sense of self-compassion and kindness, which can make staying the course feel much easier.

I wholeheartedly believe that when it comes to joyful productivity, reflection is key. That's certainly been the case for me. Returning to my example of improving my fitness: reflecting on how the process was going allowed me to realise how much I was benefitting from working out more frequently. That in turn boosted my confidence and motivation and made it easier to keep showing up for myself. But reflecting can also help us course correct when things aren't working out the way we expected them to. I often share an example of when I first started my business and set a goal for myself of hosting in-person events. I love connecting with new people and speaking on all things joy, and getting to do something I loved as part of my work felt like a real marker of success. However, when I took some time to reflect after the first few events I put on, I realised I hadn't enjoyed them as much as I'd thought I would and that doing them wasn't as aligned to my strengths as I'd first imagined. (Hosting events requires a lot of organisation, which unfortunately is not one of my super skills!) Building in that time to reflect helped me realise that I'd learnt some valuable information from taking joyful action but that, ultimately, I needed to tweak my plan to keep it feeling joyful.

Reflection is also important because the Joy Method is an iterative process. As you work towards your goals and achieve them, you will identify further changes you want to make, and taking the time to reflect and learn will give you more knowledge and information to assist you in the pursuit of those future goals. This was the case for my client Ellie. When we first started working together, her definition of success was having the freedom to travel, and we worked together on a plan for her to build a business that would allow her to work from anywhere. A few years later, we reconnected—she'd had an amazing time travelling around South America, but she was craving more stability and wanted to work towards the goal of buying her first home. By taking the time to reflect on what she'd learnt from working towards that first goal of building her business, Ellie had tonnes of tools and lessons in her back pocket to assist her as she navigated another life change.

I want to take the opportunity to share some examples of how you can apply the Joy Method in a variety of contexts. Here are a few mini case studies from my client base:

EXAMPLE 1: OLIVIA

Olivia runs a chain of baby and toddler groups, and her business has grown rapidly in the last few years. From the outside, it looked like Olivia was having great success, but that's not how it felt to her. She had started her business in order to spend more time with her own children, but as the chain grew and grew, she found herself busier than ever before. We used the Joy Method to help her make a change.

Step 1: *Define Success for You*

When we discussed what success would look and feel like for Olivia, she realised that she wanted her life to feel calmer and more balanced. She wanted to be more present for her children, and she knew that meant that she needed to outsource some elements of her business. She still cared about the health of her business, but she knew that in this season of her life, her kids were her number one priority.

Step 2: *Identify Your Strengths & Strategies*

When we started to explore what strengths or strategies Olivia had to support her in achieving her definition of success, the first thing that came to mind was her network. Olivia is a very sociable person and has built a brilliant community around her classes, and she knew that she could call on people to support her. The other thing that Olivia realised was that she works best in the mornings. For a long time she had resented her afternoon classes, but completing her energy profile helped her understand why.

Step 3: *Take Joyful Action*

Olivia identified two joyful actions she wanted to experiment with. The first was to recruit someone from her network to deliver her afternoon classes. Knowing that her mornings were her most energised time helped her see that those were the most productive hours to invest into her business, and it meant that she'd get to pick her children up from school in the afternoon and spend time with them. Olivia also decided to hand over the log-ons to her social media accounts to another one of her team members. She knew that checking her business's Instagram often pulled her focus away from her children, and this action felt like a good way of breaking that cycle.

Step 4: *Reflect & Learn*

Once Olivia had been implementing these actions for a month, we took the time in our coaching session to reflect on how they had been working for her. The changes had worked well, and Olivia realised that she wanted to be even bolder in outsourcing classes and other tasks to her team and community. Currently, she is in the process of setting up a franchise model, which will allow her to achieve her financial goals without having to sacrifice the precious time with her children.

EXAMPLE 2: SARA

Like many of my clients, Sara came to work with me because she had reached the point of burnout. She is the eldest daughter of four, and as the only one who didn't have children of her own, she had taken on the responsibility of caring for her parents, who were both experiencing ill health. This responsibility coupled with her demanding job meant that Sara ended up with very little time for herself and was exhausted as a result.

Step 1: *Define Success for You*

Sara was very clear in her definition of success: she wanted to feel like herself again. She had spent so much time giving herself over to others that she had lost sight of the things that brought her joy, and she struggled to take pleasure in tasks or activities that she had previously enjoyed. Sara wanted to recover from burnout and find her spark again, but she knew she was going to have to make some changes in order to do that.

Step 2: *Identify Your Strengths & Strategies*

When we started to explore the strengths and strategies that could help Sara to achieve her definition of success, she realised that she wanted to engage more with her strengths of creativity and appreciation of beauty to help her be more present and find delight in simple pleasures. Sara also realised that while she is great at delegating at work, she had never used this skill in her personal life and instead chose to take on extra responsibilities in order to avoid confrontation with her siblings.

Step 3: *Take Joyful Action*

Sara identified two joyful actions she wanted to experiment with. The first was to sign up for a floristry course. Sara had no aspirations to change careers, but she hoped that by committing to a course, she would be able to reconnect with her creativity and love of plants and carve out a small chunk of time each week that was just for her. The other action she identified was to speak vulnerably to her siblings about the toll caring for her parents was taking on her. Sara knew deep down that her siblings wouldn't want her to struggle, and by being open with them, she hoped they'd be able to redistribute the responsibilities more evenly.

Step 4: *Reflect & Learn*

When we took some time to reflect on the impact of Sara's actions, she was really pleased she had embarked on the floristry course. It had served the purpose of getting her in touch with her creativity again, and she had met a couple of women whom she'd got together with for a coffee outside the class. Making new friends had boosted Sara's confidence and helped her connect with who she was outside of work and her caring responsibilities.

While her siblings had been warm and responsive when she'd shared her struggles, Sara recognised that she still had some work to do in setting and maintaining boundaries. She had slipped into the role of nurturing and obedient older sister and eldest daughter for over four decades, and she acknowledged that she still had a lot of work to do in unpicking this. One of the actions she identified after this reflection was to start working with a counsellor who could help her navigate this.

I wholeheartedly believe that by using the Joy Method you can achieve whatever it is that is most important to you. And it works because it puts you at the heart of the process—your dreams, your strengths, your experiences, your abilities. The chances are that you've been ignoring or downplaying these for far too long, but not anymore. It's time to start embracing them and opening yourself up to all the joy and authentic success available to you when you do.

In the next chapter, I'll explain how we can keep your productivity archetype front and centre too. There's no one universal approach when it comes to joyful productivity, so let's throw out the rule book and do it your way. Because spoiler alert: it's the only way that actually works.

LET'S RECAP

- **The Joy Method is designed to help you make joyful changes to your life in a productive way.**
- **You can use it to achieve any goal or life change that feels important to you.**
- **It's composed of four steps: defining your version of success, identifying your strengths and strategies, taking joyful action, and reflecting and learning.**
- **The Joy Method is designed to be personalised and puts you and your needs and desires at the heart of the process.**

CHAPTER 10:

PUT THE JOY METHOD INTO ACTION

Now that you know what the Joy Method is, it's time to put it into action! In this chapter, we're going to look at the Joy Method through the lens of the four productivity archetypes, and I'm going to share lots of guidance to help you get the most from this method.

You might be wondering why it's important to think about our productivity archetypes as we dive into the Joy Method—surely the four steps are the same no matter who is using the method? Well, yes, but how we feel about each of the steps will be different depending on our productivity styles and preferences, and therefore you might need different guidance to help you get started. My hope is that by breaking the method down by archetype, I can help you release any resistance, overcome any obstacles, and get the Joy Method working for you.

You can jump ahead to the productivity archetype you most identify with, or if while reading this book you've identified with a couple of the archetypes, read each one to find the guidance that will work best for you.

The Doer

Let's start with the doer. If this is the productivity archetype you feel most aligned with, the chances are that you're chomping at the bit to just get on with the Joy Method and start taking action! However, I'd encourage you to read this section first if you want to get the most out of this process—it might just help you avoid some of the common pitfalls I see doers struggle with.

Step 1: *Define Success for You*

As someone who identifies as a doer, I know that your first instinct will be to jump straight to Step Three and start taking action. That's basically how I've approached working towards my goals for the majority of my life—having an idea and then getting straight into taking action on that idea. And that's not a bad thing. In fact, I think that having the courage and drive to persevere and move things forward is one of the most brilliant aspects of being a doer.

However, I also know from experience that if we don't take the time to pause and define success for ourselves first, we can waste a lot of energy charging down the wrong path. I did this in a big way when it came to my career, spending the best part of a decade pouring energy into promotions or achievements that I didn't really want, but I've done it in smaller ways too. For example, I've lost track of the number of times I've bought all the supplies for a new hobby before realising very quickly that it's not the thing for me.

Another reason why it's particularly important to take the time to define success on your own terms if you identify as a doer is because doers can be more prone to comparison and competition. A pattern I often see with my clients who are doers is that they will pursue goals or achievements to keep up with peers or prove that they can do something, as opposed to considering if it's going to make their lives feel more joyful or add value in any other way. Taking the time to get clear on your own definition of success will help you avoid this.

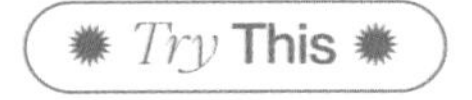

Completing the Best Possible Self exercise on page 46 will help you start crafting your definition of success, but another tool that might help is to write about what an ideal day in your life would look like. Starting from waking up in the morning until going to bed at night, jot down the tasks, activities, and experiences that you would love to fill your day with. You might even like to consider what you would be wearing and the sort of meals you would cook for yourself. As a doer, you might find this task easier than the Best Possible Self exercise, as it's focused on the action the most joyful and successful version of you would be taking.

Step 2: *Identify Your Strengths & Strategies*

Once you know what you're aiming for and have a clear sense of why you want to achieve it, the next step is to identify the strengths and strategies that will help you get there. You might already have an idea of what these are from what you've already read, but to help you, here is a bit of extra guidance tailored specifically to doers:

- Pay close attention to your own energy profile. As discussed, doers are at a high risk of pushing through and burning out, so this is a really important step. Consider when in the day you feel most energetic, how your energy responds to the different seasons, and how your hormones impact you. It might feel more productive to work around the clock and keep ticking things off the list, but as we've explored throughout this book, not respecting your body's natural rhythms and its need for rest will catch up with you eventually. Plus, you'll likely find that when you start embracing your energy profile, you'll be able to better harness your energetic high points to achieve everything you want anyway.
- Consider how you'll create more space in your schedule. Your drive to do, do, do can mean you're tempted to fill every last minute with plans or commitments, but having some quiet time is key, not only to facilitate more time for rest but also to make it easier for you to engage with your intuition. Experiment with keeping an evening each week just for yourself or trying to keep one weekend a month free of any plans.
- Resist taking on more stuff. One way to free up some more space in your schedule is to resist taking on projects and responsibilities just because you feel like you should. Doers are often the ones who will put their hands up in meetings to agree to an extra task, volunteer to help with something when they don't really want to, or take on the errands that nobody else is getting round to. And while it can be nice to help out every now and then, what we want to avoid is you adding more to your plate that distracts from the actions that really matter—the ones that move you closer to your version of success. A phrase I like to remember to help with this is *if it's not a hell yes, it's a no*—put simply, just because you can do something, doesn't mean that you necessarily should.
- Recognise that effort doesn't always equal value. Doers can often feel the need to prove themselves, and as a result, can get swept up in the idea that something being hard makes it more worthwhile. I want to remind you that that simply isn't the case, and that you can add more value when you're embracing your strengths and letting yourself have fun. Give yourself permission to lean into the easy approach, and know that the value lies in the outcome, not in how much you had to hustle to get there.

Step 3: *Take Joyful Action*

Okay, so we've finally reached the step where you'll thrive! As a fellow doer, I know that you won't need too much coaching to get started with making things happen, but there is one reminder that I want to give you before you burst into action: don't forget to ensure that the action you're taking feels joyful.

In our productivity-obsessed society, it's easy to believe that the best way of getting something done is the quickest or most efficient way, but I want you to remember that that's not true—the best way to get something done is the most joyful way. Not only will you be able to sustain your energy for longer if you're enjoying taking action, but you'll also be able to find joy in the process, minimising the chances of experiencing that arrival-fallacy dip we discussed in Chapter One.

This might feel like a new approach if you've spent your whole life up until this date trying to tick as many things off the to-do list as possible, but give it a go—you might be surprised at how much more energised it makes you feel.

Step 4: *Reflect & Learn*

Once you've started taking action, the final step is to take some time to reflect and learn. This is an easy step to miss as a doer. Once you start taking action and get that dopamine hit that comes with ticking things off the to do list, it can be tempting to keep on going instead of slowing down to reflect. But if you want to make sure you're focusing your efforts on the right things, if you're determined to keep moving in the direction of your version of success, this is a really useful step.

Here are a few key questions to consider in your reflections as a doer:

- Have my actions been moving me closer to my definition of success?
- Where am I spending most of my time and energy right now? Do I want to tweak my focus in any way?
- Where am I experiencing comparison or a desire to keep up right now? Is that urge serving me, or taking me further away from my goals?
- How does it feel to focus on joyful action? What impact is it having on my productivity?

- Where am I experiencing challenges as I take action? How can I lean into my strengths more to help me?
- Does my definition of success still feel true, or do I want to tweak it in any way?
- Is there anything else I want to note before I end my reflection?

And one surefire way to make sure you actually get round to completing your reflection? Add it to your to-do list and make sure you schedule it in your diary. As a doer, you'll struggle with seeing a task go unticked!

The Perfectionist

If you identify as a perfectionist, you might be feeling a little preoccupied with one question: How do I make sure I use the Joy Method in the right way? I've worked with lots of perfectionists in my time, and it can be this desire to get things just right that can hold them back from taking the action that will move them in the right direction. If this resonates, I've got a few pointers that will help.

Step 1: *Define Success for You*

So, let's start with our first step: defining your own version of success. One thing I've noticed in my time working with perfectionists is that they tend to be more observant than the other productivity archetypes. Perfectionists are highly detail oriented, which can be a real strength when a task requires precision. However, being so observant can also mean that perfectionists are often scanning to see what's going on around them, and they're always aware of the latest trends and standards—they need to know what "perfect" looks like in order to be able to strive to achieve it.

That constant scanning can create a bit of a challenge when it comes to creating your own definition of success. If your head is full of other people's goals or achievements, or if you're driven by meeting someone else's standards, it can be difficult to separate your authentic desires from the desires that will allow you to appear a certain way or keep up with your peers. But it's so, so important that we do create that separation. Because otherwise, you will waste your time pouring a whole load of energy and effort into something that won't actually feel good to you when you achieve it. You might already have had that experience. Maybe you landed the dream job you'd spent years working towards and still got the Sunday scaries every week. Maybe you finally saved up to take the dream vacation, only to remember that you don't actually like the beach all that much. I've worked with clients who have had these experiences and so many more, and I don't want it for you. Our time is limited—let's be sure we're making it count.

Ask yourself this question: What would I still care about if nobody was watching or judging? Often our drive for perfection is in pursuit of external validation, so taking the time to check that it's something you'd still care about even if you couldn't tell anybody about it is a great way of checking that your vision is truly authentic to you. I remember asking a client this question, and she realised that the reason why she had been pouring so much energy into her career wasn't to fulfil a personal desire but to get a "well done" from her parents. Having this realisation freed her to explore her own vision, which involved a lot more travel and a lot less racing up the career ladder.

Step 2: *Identify Your Strengths & Strategies*

The next step is to explore your strengths and strategies that can help you achieve your definition of success. Again, you might have a good sense of what these are from previous chapters, but here are a few tips and watch-outs unique to perfectionists that might help:

- Leave your modesty at the door! I find that perfectionists struggle most with claiming their strengths, particularly if they haven't been externally validated by someone else. Try to let go of the need to justify a strength and instead think about the skills and abilities that feel good to use. For example, you don't have to be Marie Kondo-levels of organised to trust that you have a knack for keeping things in order. If it feels good to organise things, claim that strength instead of worrying that you're not the most organised person alive.

- Resist trying to find the "perfect" approach. Regardless of what your goals might be, I can say with confidence that there will be more than one way that you can achieve them. It doesn't matter what path you take; what matters is that you take the action to start moving in the right direction so that you can achieve the things you truly desire. Remember that the only right way is the way that feels good to you.
- Experiment with flexibility. As we explored in Chapter Five, perfectionists can sometimes resist embracing their natural energy cycles and instead strive to perform at the same level no matter how they're feeling or what is going on in the world around them. As you may have already experienced, this is a surefire way to increase your risk of burnout and, at the very least, will expose you to negative self-talk and criticism. Instead, try to allow flexibility for different seasons—consider where you're at right now and the approach that will best serve your energetic needs, knowing that this can change in time (and trusting that this process will remind you to make that change).
- Get quiet. Remember that your intuitive thoughts and feelings are a huge strength in and of themselves, so ensure you're taking the time to slow down and connect with them every now and then in whatever way works best for you. Journaling, meditating, or simply going for a walk around the block with your phone on airplane mode can all help with this.

Step 3: *Take Joyful Action*

Once you've explored your strengths and strategies, it's time to start taking joyful action. This is where I see my clients who are perfectionists struggle the most—they can get so stuck in the previous steps that they never get round to showing up and taking the action that will make the difference. I'm going to give you the reminder that I always give them: it is much more productive to do something in an average way than to do nothing because you're worried you won't do it perfectly.

At this stage, I like to borrow a bit of jargon I learnt while working for a tech start-up. Whenever we were launching a new product, we would challenge ourselves to explore what the MVP—minimum viable product—was. We actively avoided trying to create a perfect product the first time round, because we knew that launching something and getting customer feedback would help us create a better product in the long run. The same is true for taking action—it's often only when we get going that we understand what better action would look like.

Try to take this approach, figuring out what the first tiny step could be, and then use the next step in the Joy Method to evaluate how you can make improvements next time.

Step 4: *Reflect & Learn*

Once you're on your way with taking action, the final step is to reflect on and learn from the process. One thing I want you to remember as a perfectionist is to bring a heavy dose of compassion and curiosity to this process, instead of using it as an opportunity to criticise yourself. We see with toddlers that when we shout or criticise, they freeze or rebel, whereas when we practise compassion and get curious about their behaviours, they're more likely to learn and grow. The same is true for adults—we can't discipline ourselves into joyful action. Instead, we need to bring a little bit of care and tenderness to the process so that we can grow and develop.

Here are a few key questions to consider in your reflections as a perfectionist:

- Have my actions been moving me closer to my authentic definition of success?
- What has felt good? Which actions have I enjoyed the most? Which strengths have brought me the most joy to use?
- Where am I experiencing challenges as I take action? What ideas do I have about why that might be the case?
- Have I fallen into my perfectionist tendencies at any stage? If yes, what triggered this? What might I do to avoid this next time?
- Does my definition of success still feel true, or do I want to tweak it in any way?
- What new ideas do I have that I'd like to experiment with?
- Is there anything else I want to note before I end my reflection?

And remember—there's no perfect way to complete your reflection! So long as you're taking that time-out to look back and learn the lessons, that's all that matters.

The Dreamer

If you're a dreamer, then you might already be exercising the first step of the Joy Method, dreaming up your vision for success and all the joyful changes you'll make. Before I lose you to that process, let me share some guidance for each step of the method so you have the best chances of making those dreams a reality.

Step 1: *Define Success for You*

As a dreamer, you have a natural talent for imagining a better way of doing things, which means that you'll likely be firmly in your element during this step! The chances are that your mind is already whirring from the earlier chapters and you're feeling excited about all the joyful changes you want to make.

I have only one piece of guidance for you at this stage, and it's designed to help you reduce the overwhelm during the later stages of the Joy Method: try to craft a vision of success that is specific to this season of your life.

Now, I'm not one to quash anybody's big dreams or goals—if anything, my advice is usually to dream bigger. But I've found that my clients who are dreamers struggle to marry those big lifetime goals and visions with the actions that need to be taken in the short term. So, of course, still dream big and explore all the possibilities, but then clarify what you want to achieve in the shorter term to get you on your way.

✸ *Try* **This** ✸

Figure out what success would look and feel like for you over the next three to six months. Setting a defined time period should make it much easier to figure out the strengths and strategies that will help you.

For example, say that your big long-term definition of success is to quit your corporate job and write for a living. Your short-term definition of success might be to develop a regular writing habit or to have a certain amount in your savings in order to help you manage the transition. The end dream is still the same, but by drawing the horizon in a little, it will be easier to identify the practical steps you need to take to make it a reality.

Step 2: *Identify Your Strengths & Strategies*

Once you have your long-term and shorter-term definitions of success, the next step is to get clear on the unique strengths and strategies you can employ to help you get there. Here are a few things I'd encourage you to consider at this stage:

- Let go of shame. As we discussed in Chapter Seven, we are so often made to believe that some strengths are more valuable than others, but that simply isn't the case. If you've ever felt like you needed to hide or feel ashamed of your core strengths or interests, this is your permission slip to break them out and put them to good use! The skills that often come naturally to dreamers—creativity, vulnerability, empathy, and vision, for example—are all skills that the world needs more of, and by harnessing them, you'll be able to move closer to your definition of success in a more joyful way.
- Embrace your unique energetic rhythms. Dreamers often have energetic rhythms that subvert the norms—for example, doing their best work in the evenings rather than during the day. Consider how you can use this to your advantage—is there a way for you to tweak your schedule so that you're able to focus on your biggest priorities when you're feeling most energised and creative?
- Capture your intuitive downloads. Those things that you daydream about when you're in the shower or trying to concentrate during a boring meeting? The chances are that they're downloads from your intuition. Instead of dismissing them, explore how you can capture them—perhaps you could carry a notebook around with you to jot them down, or you could talk through them with a partner or friend to see if that helps you develop the download further.
- Be mindful of distractions. When we start exploring strategies and plans, that shiny magpie syndrome can kick in, throwing up all sorts of new ideas to explore, but we'll struggle to ever enact change if we keep jumping from one idea to the next. If you're scared of forgetting the ideas that come to mind while you're working on your goals, set up a document where you can record them for a later date.

Step 3: *Take Joyful Action*

The next step in the Joy Method is to take joyful action. The biggest challenge for dreamers at this stage is knowing where to start with achieving their dreams and goals, but our earlier actions of shortening the horizon and focusing on just this season when defining success should help with that.

If you're still struggling, you might like to break the timeline down even further. Ask yourself what needs to get done this month in order to move forwards and try to give yourself the space to focus on just those things for now. This might be hard, but remember that taking action is an essential part of making your dreams a reality.

Another thing that can help if you're finding it difficult to move from dreaming and planning to actually doing is to embrace the joy available to you in the process of taking action. It will always be difficult to find the discipline and willpower to do something you don't want to do, but if we can make the tasks as enjoyable as possible, then it will be much easier to get going. And as a dreamer, you have the skills and abilities to get creative and find the fun in the process. Give yourself permission to do that, and that stage should feel a whole lot easier!

Finally, stay focused on what the action is helping you achieve. Every little step is building towards your dreamy, joyful vision for life—the more you can stay connected to that, the more motivated to take action you will feel.

Step 4: *Reflect & Learn*

The final step in the process is to reflect and learn. By taking the time to complete this step, you can strengthen your definition of success and more easily trust that your strategies and actions are moving you in the right direction. Reflecting on the progress you're making will also help you build the belief that your dreams don't have to be just dreams.

Here are a few questions that might help you reflect as a dreamer:

- What actions have I taken to move closer to my definition of success?
- How does it feel to see the progress I've been making?
- Have I gone offtrack at any point? If so, what can I change to stay focused on action?

- Are there any new ideas or dreams that I'd like to fold into my definition of success?
- Where have I used my strengths? How has it felt to do so?
- Is there anything else I want to note before I end my reflection?

You can complete your reflections any way you'd like, but again, remember to think about how you can bring your strengths and strategies to the process. Do you feel more inspired to reflect if you can turn it into a creative task, or are you more likely to have the headspace to do so at a particular time? Considering these things can help you take more from the process.

The Procrastinator

Finally, if you identify as a procrastinator, you might already be thinking about how to avoid the Joy Method. In fact, you might even be tempted to skip to the end of this book or close it completely. I urge you not to do that. You have picked up this book for a reason, and I want to help you make the changes that will add more joy to your life. Just because you've struggled to make those changes in the past doesn't mean that you always will, and I've got some tips and pointers to help you make the Joy Method work for you.

Step 1: *Define Success for You*

The official first step of the Joy Method is to define your own version of success, but if you identify as a procrastinator, I've got a little pre-step that I'd like you to do first. Here it is: accept that change is possible. Even if that feels hard to believe right now, suspend disbelief for as long as it takes you to work through the Joy Method, just once.

I've worked with quite a few procrastinators as a coach, and I also sometimes identify as a procrastinator myself (maybe even in the process of writing this book . . .). I know that, often, the biggest hurdle to overcome is shifting the mindset that tells us there's no point, as it's not going to work anyway. Let me let you in on a secret: If you've ever had that thought, it's not because you don't have what it takes to make the changes you desire. It's just your brain trying to keep you safe.

You see, thinking about working towards a goal or making a change comes with a risk. There's the risk that we might try something new and fail, and we might have to deal with the discomfort and embarrassment that would bring. But there's also the risk that we might be wildly successful and get everything we've ever wanted. Both of these present a threat to our brain, which values predictability and certainty over anything else. That's why we often find ourselves reaching for the statements or beliefs that keep us stuck in one place or procrastinating with activities or tasks that feel less risky.

I've found that often just knowing that our default response to fear is to stay stuck where we are can be enough to shift out of that pattern. The other thing that can really help is to become so familiar with our vision of success that it feels less terrifying to our brain, meaning we're less likely to self-sabotage.

✹ *Try* This ✹

Don't just craft your own definition of success, get cosy with it. I want you to spend some time imagining how it would feel to live the version of your life that would bring you the most joy. I want you to envisage how your days would look, to try this new life on for size. The part of your brain that controls fear and emotion can't tell the difference between something that is real and imagined (hence why we often find ourselves crying at books or movies), which is why the more you expose yourself to this future vision, the less scary and overwhelming it will seem.

Step 2: *Identify Your Strengths & Strategies*

Once you've accepted that you can make a change, crafted your definition of success, and started to get familiar with it, the next step is to identify the strengths and strategies that can help you get there. You should hopefully have a few ideas for this step already from the previous chapters, but here are a few extra pointers that might be extra helpful for procrastinators:

- Maximise your productivity sweet spot. If you identify as a procrastinator, it's important that you take the path of least resistance when it comes to making a change or achieving a goal. One of the ways you can do that is to get clear on when your energetic high points happen and harness them for taking action. Revisit Chapter Five or look back at the energy profile you made in Chapter Nine, and identify the time of day or month when you feel most focused and energised. Then make sure you plan your actions for those periods of time to give yourself the best chance of success. (Side note: this isn't a permission slip to procrastinate until your favourite season rolls around!)

- Press pause on the stuff that isn't a priority. A crafty strategy I often see my procrastinator clients adopt is taking on more of the tasks that feel safe to them in order to have a legitimate excuse to avoid the stuff that feels scarier. For example, my client Lisa knew that she really wanted to change her career and had a clear plan of how she could do that, but she kept volunteering to host family events or help out at her daughter's school, leaving her with little time to work on the course she was taking as part of her retraining. You're never going to make the progress you desire if you're always filling your schedule, so press pause on the stuff that isn't a priority for now.

- Get your environment right. In my experience supporting procrastinators, I've found that they're often more sensitive to outside influences than the other productivity archetypes. If that rings true, think about whom or what you need in your environment to help you be successful. For example, while I was writing this book, I found it really useful to have my friend be my accountability buddy. We meet for a walk or a playdate every week with our daughters, and knowing that she'd ask me how many words I'd written or how I was getting on gave me an extra burst of focus when I could feel myself getting distracted. Additionally, I know I work better when I'm sitting at my desk as opposed to working from a café or another room in my house, and so I tried to create as many opportunities to be at my desk as possible, even if it was just for half an hour in the evening once I'd put my little one to bed.

Step 3: *Take Joyful Action*

Once you've identified the things that will help you create the path of least resistance and show up for your goals, the next step is to start taking joyful action. One thing I've noticed from supporting procrastinators in my work is that they often have a desire to know the whole plan before taking action. If that feels familiar to you, know that trying to figure out the whole plan before you begin is just another way of procrastinating and keeping yourself safe.

You don't need to have every step mapped out in order to take action. You just need to know what the first step will be. Then once you've completed that first step, you can take some time to figure out the next step. Plus, it's often from taking action that we're able to clarify what the next steps will be. For example, when I first started writing this book, I didn't know every single thing I wanted to include in it. But once I'd written Chapter One, I had a much clearer idea, and after writing Chapter Nine, I'd covered things I would never have thought about before I got stuck in.

Remember also to pay attention to the joyful part of this step. You'll find it much easier to show up if you know you're going to enjoy the process of taking the action. For example, if you have a goal of improving your fitness, you might find it much easier to go for a hike with a friend than hit the gym. Doing the thing will always be more productive than not doing the thing, and cranking up the enjoyment factor will always produce better results than trying to discipline yourself into doing something.

Step 4: *Reflect & Learn*

The final step of the Joy Method is to take the time to reflect and learn. This is a really important step for procrastinators, as it will help you see the progress you're making, which will help you build the belief that you can achieve your definition of success. And if when you pause to reflect you realise that you haven't taken the action you hoped you would, having the right mindset can help you learn valuable information that will help you in the next iteration. The key is to be curious, not critical—act like a detective looking for clues as to why you've resisted action, instead of like a strict school teacher handing out insults.

Here are a few questions that you can use to help shape your reflections if you identify as a procrastinator:

- What actions have I taken to move closer to my definition of success?
- What beliefs am I challenging by showing up and taking action?
- Have I found myself stuck at any point? If so, what can I change to help me stay focused on taking action?
- How does it feel to focus on joyful action? What impact is it having on my productivity?

- Does my definition of success still feel true, or do I want to tweak it in any way?
- Is there anything else I want to note before I end my reflection?

If you're worried that you might procrastinate on completing your reflection, consider some of the strategies we discussed earlier. Could you set up a coffee date with a friend or colleague to talk this through? Is there an environment where you feel particularly reflective that might help reduce any resistance you're experiencing? Use what you know about yourself and how you're motivated to make it happen.

Navigating Resistance

It's important to acknowledge that taking this approach might feel strange or even unsafe to you if you have been conditioned to please other people or believe that certain goals are more worthy than others. It might feel hard to embrace your strengths if you struggle with low self-esteem, and you might find it tricky to trust that allowing yourself to enjoy the process can be as fruitful as relying on discipline and hard work. I have worked with many clients who have experienced the same resistance over the years, and I'm going to share with you the same reminder that I share with them: you have tried to do it the old way for a long time, and it hasn't worked.

I'm not asking you to commit to the Joy Method forever—I'm simply inviting you to give it a go and see if it works for you. Here are a few things that might help:

- Consider who you want to set a positive example for. If you have people in your life who look up to you in any way, whether that be children, colleagues, or friends, remember that by embracing the Joy Method and focusing on your own definition of joy and success you are modelling that it is safe to do the same thing. So many of us want our loved ones to be happy, but we don't grant ourselves the same permission slip—and in doing so, what we actually demonstrate to them is that they, too, must hustle and sacrifice their well-being.
- Share the Joy Method with a friend. Committing to implementing this method with a pal will hopefully make it feel less intimidating and more like a fun experiment you're conducting together. You could set up some

coffee dates to check in with your experiences or simply drop each other a text every now and then to stay accountable.

- Start small. If you're feeling dubious about the impact the Joy Method could have, start small. Pick a tiny change in your life and see if the method can help you bring it to fruition. If that works, you can then try using the Joy Method on more transformative changes, safe in the knowledge that you're not wasting your time or energy.
- Get started right now! It's tempting when reading a book to put it to one side and trust that you'll come back to the exercises and actions at a later date, but in my experience, it's rare that we actually do. While you're reading this, do something to get you started with the Joy Method, whether it's envisaging your best possible future life or making a note of your core strengths. The first step is always the most difficult, but once you've started, you'll have some positive momentum behind you.

I hope that whatever your productivity archetype, you're feeling armed and ready to get started with the Joy Method. I have seen this approach change the game for my clients, and it's helped me achieve so many of my own joyful goals, both big and small. And the reason it works? Because it captures the very essence of you, and uses that to get things done, rather than encourages you to conform to an approach or way of being that doesn't feel right.

I am such a big believer that when women show up as they are and embrace their strengths and uniqueness, magic happens. For too long now, we've been taught to hide our quirks and difference instead of harnessing them, and we've suffered as a result. It's time to start focusing our time and energy on the stuff that really matters and find some joy along the way. I hope that the Joy Method will help you do just that.

A MANIFESTO FOR A NEW WAY OF DOING THINGS

> Tell me, what else should I have done?
>
> Doesn't everything die at last, and too soon?
>
> Tell me, what is it you plan to do
>
> with your one wild and precious life?
>
> —Mary Oliver, "The Summer Day"

Throughout this book, I've made a case for approaching productivity differently. I hope it's inspired you to rethink how you measure your worth, how you value your time and energy, and how you decide what's important to you in this one wild and precious life that we are lucky enough to have been given.

As we come to the end of our journey together, I want to leave you with a manifesto—a set of guiding principles that encapsulates the essence of joyful productivity and the key lessons we've explored throughout this book.

Here goes . . .

1) The only version of success that matters is yours.

Trust me when I say that there is no number of achievements that can plug the gap if you're chasing somebody else's definition of success. It doesn't matter how proud your parents are or how many likes you receive on LinkedIn or how many people tell you that you're doing great—it will feel hollow if it's not truly what you want.

Take the time to find your most honest definition of success. Examine it, question it, look for where other people's expectations of you might be creeping in. When you have a definition of success that feels authentic and truthful to you, you have what so many of us desire—a path to follow that will feel fulfilling and purposeful.

2) Build an identity that is about more than just your achievements.

When someone asks you who you are, have something to tell them other than your job title. You are so much more than your achievements or what you do to earn money. You are your thoughts and your beliefs and your interests. You are the way you express your love and the way you care for others. You are a vessel for joy, and laughter, and grief, and hope, and sadness, and limitless amounts of love.

Living a rich life requires you to embrace and nurture all the different parts of yourself—your hobbies, your relationships, your curiosities. Remember that you are a human, not just a machine.

3) Quit the comparison game.

Don't waste your one wild and precious life trying to keep pace with anybody else. Their definition of success might be vastly different from yours. They might not even know what their definition of success is. Comparison is not just the thief of joy, it is the thief of focus and intention. It really doesn't matter what anybody else is doing. It matters that you're moving in the direction that feels great to you.

Reject the pressure to compete. Competing with other women is one of the many ways that the patriarchy gets us to do its dirty work—and it only adds to the fiction that we can do it all. Instead, share your truth, and listen to what your loved ones share in return. You might just find that things feel a little lighter as a result.

4) Challenge your inner critic.

When things feel challenging, take a beat before you let your inner critic run wild. You're not lazy or weak or undisciplined—you're simply a woman trying to navigate a world that wasn't made with you in mind. The chances are that you are managing an unrelenting and ever-growing load that is added to by gender norms, sexism, and societal expectations. It feels hard because it is hard.

When we accept that, we can show ourselves more compassion and kindness. It's already tough enough out there—don't add your own self-blame to the pile of crap you have to carry.

5) Adopt an attitude of embracing rather than fixing.

If you're anything like me, you might have grown up feeling like a project to be fixed. Always believing that your "real life" would start once you'd fixed all your flaws and bad habits, that happiness would arrive once you were thinner, or smarter, or busier, or better organised. That things would finally click once you just managed to bend to someone else's routine or plan.

I call bullshit on that. The most productive thing you can do is to embrace who you truly are—to supercharge your strengths, to ride your energetic ebbs and flows, to find the blend that works for you. Lean into who you are and away from who you think you "should" be. You'll find some magic there when you do.

6) Know that just because you can doesn't mean you should.

This is a piece of advice I come back to all the time. If you're a people pleaser or you've always felt like you have something to prove, the chances are that you might say yes or choose to do something for reasons that don't have your best interests at heart.

Before setting a goal or adding something new to your plate, try to check in with your intuition. If the idea of doing the thing doesn't feel like a huge yes, let it be a no. You don't need to prove yourself to anybody but yourself. There is real beauty and power in surrendering what is not for you.

7) Harness the power of future regret.

There is only one thing that we are guaranteed in this life, and that's that one day it will end. Even if we have decades still left to live, our time here is finite and always depleting. That can be depressing to accept, but it can also be an incredible catalyst for joyful productivity. When you remember that none of us is getting out of here alive, it makes striving for someone else's goals feel entirely redundant.

The chances are that when the end inevitably comes, it won't be the nights you stayed late at the office or the accolades you collected that you remember fondly. It will be the memories you made with your loved ones, the joyful moments you experienced, the times you felt inspired and connected. Try to remember that as you plan your time.

8) Celebrate your wins.

I'm going to make a bold statement here: I have never met a woman who celebrates herself enough. We shy away from celebrating our wins, afraid that it will make us seem arrogant or unlikeable, and it's no surprise—we exist in a culture that raises boys to be confident and assertive, while girls are expected to be humble and nurturing.

But here's the thing: what gets recognised gets repeated. When we take a moment to pause and celebrate our wins, we build motivation and focus that makes showing up for our authentic goals feel so much easier. Plus, putting some focus on what we've already done rather than being completely absorbed by what is still left to do can help create some breathing room.

9) Be in the season you're in.

One of the most valuable things I've learnt in the process of writing this book is that life comes with many different seasons and that one of the simplest things we can do to boost our productivity is to be in the season we're in. If you're at a part of your cycle when you feel more introspective and reflective, focus on the tasks on your to-do list that could benefit from that introspection. If you're in a season of life where you're already stretched thinly, accept that maybe now is not the time to add another taxing goal.

We waste so much energy trying to push against our realities, but we don't need to. Just like trying to grow strawberries in the dead of winter would be a futile endeavour, so, too, is trying to ignore the season of life we're in. It's much more productive (and so much more joyful!) to embrace rather than resist.

10) Lean into what feels good.

And finally, the little mantra that I utter to myself more than any other: *lean into what feels good*. As women, we have a greater resistance to feeling good. We tell ourselves that it is better to feel selfless or helpful or productive or busy, but the truth is that feeling good is a superpower. When we feel good, everything gets better, from our work to our relationships, from our health to our resilience.

Take the easeful option, sprinkle some magic over the mundane, let yourself have some fun. Joy is a radical act, but especially so if you are a woman or belong to any other marginalised group. Seize it.

CONCLUSION

When I first had the idea for this book back in the summer of 2022, I knew that it would be an interesting topic to explore. But it was only during the process of researching and writing it that I realised just how much I needed this book.

As it took shape and unfolded, so, too, did a new chapter of my life. There's the obvious change—becoming a mother—and all that has meant for my identity, ambitions, and definition of success. But there's more to it than just that. I sit firmly within my mid-thirties now, and things feel different here. As a millennial woman, raised to be ambitious in my quest for gender equality and told that there was nothing I couldn't do, I have always felt the pressure to have it all. But that pressure has never felt as heavy as it does right now. The "all" has never encompassed so many parts.

Every single day, I am sold the idea that success for a woman my age is to simultaneously be able to raise a perfect family, forge a trailblazing career, and keep an immaculate home. Extra points if you can also adhere to all of society's beauty ideals in the process. Every single day, as I scroll Instagram or watch TV or read a magazine, I'm shown how highly celebrated the women who achieve all those things are. But what I don't see so much in the media is the reality that sits behind that shiny facade.

I don't see the confusion and uncertainty that arises when deciding whether to start a family, or the fertility struggles and painful losses that greet so many of those who do. I don't see the self-criticism that builds as our bodies and faces start to change, or the sadness and stress that come with having to care for ageing parents. I don't see the misogynistic barriers or logistical challenges that have to be pushed through in order to maintain and progress our careers, or the impacts of our hormonal fluctuations on our energy and our mood. I don't see the toll all these things take on our confidence and self-worth. Is it any wonder that so many of us get stuck in a cycle of comparison and striving, never feeling like we're doing enough? Is it any wonder so many of us are experiencing burnout?

If you take just one thing away from this book, I hope that it's this: success is not about having it all; it's about having what matters most to you. It isn't sustainable to keep striving to meet society's ideals without acknowledging our own unique contexts, and it isn't productive either. Because what I value and hope for in my life might be wildly different from what you value and hope for.

It doesn't serve any of us to compare or pit ourselves against one another, and it isn't helpful to believe that there's a single answer or plan or schedule that will work for us all. We are all unique, and it's significantly more productive (and much more joyful!) to acknowledge and embrace that rather than to try to mould ourselves to fit some nuclear way of life.

Before I had my daughter, I was adamant that my career would be just as important to me once I became a mother. In fact, I thought it was my moral imperative as a feminist to remain as ambitious as ever even as I took on this new role. What I can see now, fourteen months into juggling work and motherhood, is that my priorities have shifted. I still love my work, I still care about doing a good job, but my focus is less singular. There are other things in my life that require my attention right now, other areas in which I want to develop and grow. Researching this book has given me the confidence to know that that's more than okay. Seasons change—what matters isn't that we march on like robots, never being impacted by the changes in our lives, but that we are intentional in how we're spending our time and energy, channelling it into the things we value the most instead of wasting it trying to keep up with other people's ideals or our previous definitions of success. That's true productivity.

I hope this book has given you the courage to embrace whatever season of life you find yourself in. I hope it has given you the confidence to stop looking to others for all the answers, and the tools you need to find them inside of yourself instead. They have always been there. They might just have been drowned out by other people's expectations and opinions and advice. Above all, I hope this book has shown you that you were never weak or lazy or unmotivated—you were just simply trying to play a game that was rigged. And I hope it's given you a few Super Mario-style power-ups that help you tackle it more joyfully moving forwards.

I want to leave you with one last reminder: you are already enough. You are a magnificent, unique, resilient, love-filled human, and it is a miracle that you exist. You have nothing to prove and everything to enjoy. Don't waste this one wild and precious life of yours believing that happiness is waiting for you further down the line. Seize it now. I will be rooting for you every single step of the way.

ACKNOWLEDGEMENTS

As I hope you have gathered, the subject of this book is something I'm incredibly passionate about. Thank you to my wonderful publisher, Blue Star Press, for giving me the opportunity and resources to explore it. This is the third project we have worked on together, and I couldn't wish for a happier home for my words.

Thank you to every member of the team who has contributed to bringing this book to life. It feels unfair that my name is the only one on the spine when so many people have worked so hard on it. Particular thanks to Avalon Radys and Lindsay Wilkes-Edrington for all your hard work helping me untangle the ideas in my head and shape them into something compelling. Thanks also to Nancy Peske for your thoughtful edits and builds.

Thank you to my wonderful colleague, Katie Chesworth, for helping me keep all the plates spinning throughout my pregnancy and maternity leave and while writing this book. This work would feel a lot less joyful without you.

Thank you to my wonderful clients and community who have informed so much of what I wrote about in this book. Helping you achieve your definition of success is a privilege I don't take for granted.

To my friends—from the ones I've known since I was a teenager to the mum pals who I've met only in the last few years—thank you for the WhatsApp check-ins, the playdates, the pep talks, and your endless patience while I've navigated the most full-on period of my life. I love you, and I'm so glad I get to navigate this chapter and all the chapters still to come with such incredible women by my side.

To my family—especially my parents, Jane and Tony; my sister, Molly; and my in-laws, Diana and Paul—thank you for everything. Your unwavering support, encouragement, and belief has been the biggest gift in these last few years, and this book wouldn't exist without your practical help either. To Ralf, Lyla, and Poppy, you inspire me every day.

And finally, the biggest thank-you to my team at home, Sam and Seren. Sam—while researching this book, I read that one of the greatest productivity hacks was to marry the right person. I concur. None of this would be possible if you weren't so willing to share the load. I am so grateful for you. Seren—you have already taught me so much about success and joy and about what really matters. I thank my lucky stars every single day that I get to be your mum, and I can't wait for all the adventures still to come.

BIBLIOGRAPHY

Alex M. Wood, P. Alex Linley, John Maltby, Todd B. Kashdan, and Robert Hurling. "Using Personal and Psychological Strengths Leads to Increases in Well-Being over Time: A Longitudinal Study and the Development of the Strengths Use Questionnaire." *Personality and Individual Differences* 50, no. 1 (2011): 15–9. https://doi.org/10.1016/j.paid.2010.08.004.

Ambady, Nalini. "The Perils of Pondering: Intuition and Thin Slice Judgments." In "Special Issue on Intuition," special issue, *Psychological Inquiry* 21, no. 4 (2010): 271–78. https://www.jstor.org/stable/25767201.

Archer, Simon N., Donna L Robilliard, Debra J Skene, Marcel Smits, Adrian Williams, Josephine Arendt, and Malcolm von Schantz. "A Length Polymorphism in the Circadian Clock Gene Per3 is Linked to Delayed Sleep Phase Syndrome and Extreme Diurnal Preference." *SLEEP* 26, no. 4 (2003): 413–5. https://doi.org/10.1093/sleep/26.4.413.

Barua, Akrur. "Gender Equality, Dealt a Blow by COVID-19, Still Has Much Ground to Cover." *Deloitte Insights*. Jan 21, 2022. https://www2.deloitte.com/uk/en/insights/economy/impact-of-covid-on-women.html.

Bellezza, Silvia, Neeru Paharia, and Anat Keinan. "Conspicuous Consumption of Time: When Busyness and Lack of Leisure Time Become a Status Symbol." *Journal of Consumer Research* 44, no. 2 (2017): 118–38. https://doi.org/10.1093/jcr/ucw076.

Ben-Shahar, Tal. "You Accomplished Something Great: So Now What?." *New York Times,* May 28, 2019. https://www.nytimes.com/2019/05/28/smarter-living/you-accomplished-something-great-so-now-what.html.

Beverley, Grace. *Working Hard, Hardly Working: How to Achieve More, Stress Less and Feel Fulfilled*. London: Penguin, 2021.

British Chambers of Commerce. "BCC Launches Three-Year Gender Equity Campaign Based on Stark Research Findings." Mar 7, 2023. https://www.britishchambers.org.uk/news/2023/03/bcc-launches-three-year-gender-equity-campaign-based-on-stark-research-findings/.

BMJ. "Doctors' 'Gut Feeling' Should Not Be Ignored." Press release. Sep 25, 2012. https://www.bmj.com/press-releases/2012/09/25/doctors%E2%80%99-%E2%80%9Cgut-feeling%E2%80%9D-should-not-be-ignored.

Brown, Brené. *Atlas of the Heart: Mapping Meaningful Connection and the Language of Human Experience*. Toronto, ON: Vermillion, an imprint of Penguin Random House, 2021.

Calm. "What Your Chronotype Says About Your Sleep Patterns, Productivity and Personality." Mar 26, 2024. https://www.calm.com/blog/sleep-chronotypes.

Cameron, Julia. *The Artist's Way: A Spiritual Path to Higher Creativity*. London: Souvenir Press, an imprint of Profile Books, 2020.

Cawley, John. "The Impact of Obesity on Wages." *The Journal of Human Resources* 39, no. 2 (2004): 451–74. https://doi.org/10.2307/3559022.

Choi-Allum, Lona. "Understanding a Changing Older Workforce: An Examination of Workers Ages 40–Plus." AARP Research, Jan 18, 2023. https://www.aarp.org/content/dam/aarp/research/surveys_statistics/econ/2023/value-of-experience-age-discrimination-infographic.doi.10.26419-2Fres.00554.014.pdf.

Cotter, Katherine N., and James O. Pawelski. "Art Museums as Institutions for Human Flourishing." *Journal of Positive Psychology* (2021): 288–302. https://doi.org/10.1080/17439760.2021.2016911.

Csikszentmihalyi, Mihaly. *Flow: The Psychology of Optimal Experience*. New York: Harper and Row, 1989.

Dalton-Smith, Saundra. "The Real Reason Why We Are Tired and What to Do About It." Filmed Mar 2019 in Atlanta. TED video, 9:33. https://www.ted.com/talks/saundra_dalton_smith_the_real_reason_why_we_are_tired_and_what_to_do_about_it.

Dane, Erik. "When Should I Trust My Gut? Linking Domain Expertise to Intuitive Decision-Making Effectiveness." *Organizational Behavior and Human Decision Processes* 119, no. 2 (2012): 187–94. https://doi.org/10.1016/j.obhdp.2012.07.009.

Doyle, Glennon. *Untamed: Stop Pleasing, Start Living*. Random House, 2021.

Durham University. "Rest and Well-Being: World's Largest Survey." Science Daily. Sep 28, 2016. https://www.sciencedaily.com/releases/2016/09/160928153541.htm.

Edge Foundation. "ADHD and Estrogen." Accessed May 9, 2024. https://edge-foundation.org/adhd-and-estrogen/.

Endometriosis UK. n.d. "Endometriosis Facts and Figures." Accessed May 9, 2024. https://www.endometriosis-uk.org/endometriosis-facts-and-figures.

Fischer, Agneta H., Mariska E. Kret, Joost Broekens. "Gender Differences in Emotion Perception and Self-Reported Emotional Intelligence: A Test of the Emotion Sensitivity Hypothesis." *PLOS One* 13, no. 1 (2018): e0190712. https://doi.org/10.1371/journal.pone.0190712.

Fredrickson, Barbara L. "The Broaden-and-Build Theory of Positive Emotions." *Philosophical Transactions of the Royal Society B* 359, 1449 (2004): 1367–77. http://doi.org/10.1098/rstb.2004.1512.

Future Forum. "Amid Spiking Burnout, Workplace Flexibility Fuels Company Culture and Productivity: Winter Snapshot." Future Forum Pulse. Feb 2023. https://futureforum.com/research/future-forum-pulse-winter-2022-2023-snapshot/.

Gallup. "Employees Who Use Their Strengths Outperform Those Who Don't." Oct 8, 2015. https://www.gallup.com/workplace/236561/employees-strengths-outperform-don.aspx.

Gallup. "How to Build Better Teams in the Workplace." Accessed May 9, 2024. https://www.gallup.com/cliftonstrengths/en/278225/how-to-improve-teamwork.aspx.

Goldstein, Andrea N., Stephanie M. Greer, Jared M. Saletin, Allison G. Harvey, Jack B. Nitschke, and Matthew P. Walker. "Tired and Apprehensive: Anxiety Amplifies the Impact of Sleep Loss on Aversive Brain Anticipation." *Journal of Neuroscience* 33, no. 26 (2013): 10607–15. https://doi.org/10.1523/JNEUROSCI.5578-12.2013.

Hill, Maisie. *Period Power: Harness Your Hormones and Get Your Cycle Working for You*. London: Green Tree, an imprint of Bloomsbury, 2019.

International Foundation of Employee Benefit Plans. "The Importance of Taking Annual Leave." The CPD Certification Service. Jul 18, 2023. https://cpduk.co.uk/news/the-importance-of-taking-annual-leave.

Kessler, Ronald C. "Insomnia and the Performance of US Workers: Results from the America Insomnia Survey." *SLEEP* 34, no. 9 (2011): 1161–71. https://doi.org/10.5665/SLEEP.1230.

Keynes, John Maynard. "Economic Possibilities for our Grandchildren." In *Essays in Persuasion*, 358–73. New York: W.W. Norton & Co., 1963.

King, Laura A. "The Health Benefits of Writing About Life Goals." *Personality and Social Psychology Bulletin* 27, no. 7 (2001): 798–807. https://doi.org/10.1177/0146167201277003.

Lichterman, Gabrielle. "The Female Hormone Cycle." Hormonology. Accessed May 9, 2024. https://www.myhormonology.com/learn/female-hormone-cycle/.

Lichterman, Gabrielle. "The Male Hormone Cycle." Hormonology. Accessed May 9, 2024. https://www.myhormonology.com/learn/male-hormone-cycle/.

Lyubomirsky, S., L. King, and E. Diener. "The Benefits of Frequent Positive Affect: Does Happiness Lead to Success?." *Psychological Bulletin* 131, no. 6 (2005): 803–55. http://dx.doi.org/10.1037/0033-2909.131.6.803.

Mallampalli, Monica P., and Christine L. Carter. "Exploring Sex and Gender Differences in Sleep Health: A Society for Women's Health Research Report." *Journal of Women's Health* 23, no. 7 (2014): 553–62. https://doi.org/10.1089/jwh.2014.4816.

McLean, Carmen P., Anu Asnaani, Brett T. Litz, and Stefan G. Hofmann. "Gender Differences in Anxiety Disorders: Prevalence, Course of Illness, Comorbidity and Burden of Illness." *Journal of Psychiatric Research* 45, no. 8 (2011): 1027–35. https://doi.org/10.1016/j.jpsychires.2011.03.006.

Nagoski, Emily, and Amelia Nagoski. *Burnout: Solve Your Stress Cycle*. Vermillion, an imprint of Penguin Random House, 2020.

OECD. Social Protection and Well-Being: Gender. Last modified Feb 18, 2021. Distributed by OECD.Stat. https://stats.oecd.org/Index.aspx?dataset-code=TIME_USE#, time-use survey.

Peterson, C., M.E.P. Seligman. *Character strengths and virtues: A handbook and classification*. Oxford University Press/American Psychological Association, 2004.

Peterson Gloor, Jamie L., Tyler G. Okimoto, and Eden B. King. "'Maybe Baby?' The Employment Risk of Potential Parenthood." In "Revisioning, Rethinking, Restructuring Gender at Work." In special issue, *Journal of Applied Social Psychology* (Aug 2022): 623–42. https://doi.org/10.1111/jasp.12799.

Reese, Hope. "The Gendering of Holiday Labor." JSTOR Daily. Dec 21, 2019. https://daily.jstor.org/the-gendering-of-holiday-labor/.

Samson, David R., Alyssa N. Crittenden, Ibrahim A. Mabulla, Audax Z. P. Mabulla, and Charles L. Nunn. "Chronotype Variation Drives Night-Time Sentinel-Like Behaviour in Hunter-Gatherers." *Proceedings of the Royal Society B* 284 (2017): 20170967. https://doi.org/10.1098/rspb.2017.0967.

Sandberg, Sheryl. *Lean In: Women, Work, and the Will to Lead*. London: W.H. Allen, an imprint of Penguin Random House, 2013.

Seidler, Aileen, Katy Sarah Weihrich, Frederik Bes, Jan de Zeeuw, and Dieter Kunz. "Seasonality of Human Sleep: Polysomnographic Data of a Neuropsychiatric Sleep Clinic." In "Sleep and Circadian Rhythms," *Frontiers in Neuroscience* 17 (2023). https://doi.org/10.3389/fnins.2023.1105233.

Seo, Hannah. "What Does It Mean to Be Likable – and Who Has to Abide by Those Rules?." *The Guardian*. Dec 18, 2023. https://www.theguardian.com/wellness/2023/dec/18/likability-women-people-of-color-gender-bias.

Tews, Michael J., Kathryn Stafford, and Jinfei Zhu. "Beauty Revisited: The Impact of Attractiveness, Ability, and Personality in the Assessment of Employment Suitability." *International Journal of Selection and Assessment* 17, no. 1 (2009): 92–100. https://doi.org/10.1111/j.1468-2389.2009.00454.x.

Ware, Bronnie. *The Top Five Regrets of the Dying: A Life Transformed by the Dearly Departing*. 2nd ed. Carlsbad, CA: Hay House UK, 2019.

Bao, Wei, Yunhong Wang, Tingting Yu, Jiarong Zhou, Junlong Luo. "Women Rely on "Gut Feeling"? The Neural Pattern of Gender Difference in Non-Mathematic Intuition." *Personality and Individual Differences* 196 (2022): 111720. https://doi.org/10.1016/j.paid.2022.111720.

ABOUT THE AUTHOR

Sophie Cliff is a qualified coach and positive psychology practitioner. In 2018, she founded The Joyful Coach Ltd, a business dedicated to helping individuals and companies discover purpose and joy. Today, Sophie reaches people worldwide through her coaching, speaking, and workshops.

Sophie holds an MSc in applied positive psychology and coaching psychology from the University of East London. She is the author of the book *Choose Joy* and the card deck *Sprinkles of Joy*, as well as the host of the chart-topping podcast *Practical Positivity*.

Sophie lives in Leeds, United Kingdom, with her husband and daughter. When she's not helping people find more joy, she enjoys reading brilliant books, hiking in the countryside, and spending time with her family.

Other titles by Sophie Cliff:

CHOOSE JOY

SPRINKLES OF JOY